Disciplining and drafting, or 21st century learning?

Rethinking the New Zealand senior secondary curriculum for the future

Rachel Bolstad and Jane Gilbert

NZCER PRESS
Wellington 2008

NZCER PRESS
New Zealand Council for Educational Research
PO Box 3237
Wellington
New Zealand

© NZCER, 2008

ISBN 978-1-877398-35-3

All rights reserved

Designed by Cluster Creative

Printed by Lithoprint, Wellington

Distributed by NZCER Distribution Services
PO Box 3237
Wellington
New Zealand
www.nzcer.org.nz

Contents

Acknowledgements	5
Introduction: Senior secondary schooling and 21st century learning—issues and questions	7
PART 1 The changing landscape of senior secondary education in New Zealand	**11**
Introduction	12
The traditional senior curriculum—where did it come from?	14
New pressures and changes in the education landscape	22
1. Increased retention rates	23
2. Expansion of the tertiary sector	26
3. Changes to school qualifications and assessment systems	29
4. Emphasis on student 'pathways' and 'transitions' from school	32
5. The Knowledge Society and 21st century learning	35
The senior secondary school today—education for the 21st century?	41

PART 2 The senior curriculum in New Zealand today—frameworks, structures, and standards	**49**
The regulatory frameworks for the New Zealand Curriculum	50
The pre-1990s senior secondary curriculum	51
The introduction of the 1990s New Zealand Curriculum	52
The introduction of NCEA	53
The national curriculum documents and the Years 11–13 'school' curriculum	58
The school curriculum	62
The assessed curriculum	67
Unit Standards	68
Achievement Standards	71
Plus ça change, plus c'est la même chose …	77
PART 3 Where to from here? Some options for the future	**79**
The senior secondary curriculum since 1990—four key themes	80
Developing a 21st century senior school curriculum: first steps	92
Rethinking the discipline–curriculum relationship for 21st century secondary schools	95
Model 1: Mass customisation—extrapolating and refining the status quo	118
Model 2: Diverse suppliers—extending the market model	120
Model 3: Joining up supply and demand—developing 'prosumers'	121
The way ahead?	123
References	**125**
Appendices	
NCEA Achievement Standards (as at November 2006)	134
Appendix B: Approved subjects list for entrance to university (as at December 2005)	135

Acknowledgements

In preparing this work we received a great deal of support from many people. In particular, we would like to acknowledge the support of two of our colleagues at NZCER, Robyn Baker and Rosemary Hipkins, for their work in reading and critically commenting on the many drafts, and Robyn Baker for the resources and support that allowed us to complete this work (and also for her continued insistence that we do it!).

We would also like to acknowledge the support of the Ministry of Education. Some of the material that informed this work was compiled by Rachel Bolstad for a background paper on the current state of the senior secondary curriculum (in New Zealand, and other similar countries) commissioned by the Ministry in 2006. However, this material has, since then, been substantially reshaped, and new material and new ideas added that may or may not fit with current Ministry policy. We would like to acknowledge the contribution of several Ministry of Education staff who provided us with information and directed us to key sources for this earlier work: in particular,

Mary Chamberlain, Ann Greenaway, Steve Benson, Geoff Gibbs, Ben Long, Robyn Smits, Caroline Hodge, Maryanne Mills, Sandra Cubitt, Melba Scott, Alison Dow, Anne Alkema, Camilla Highfield, and Elizabeth Eppel. Thanks are also due to David Phillips (then of NZQA) and Andy Begg (of AUT University) for providing us with additional information about senior secondary curriculum and assessment in New Zealand. However, the way this information has been assembled, and any errors of fact that may remain, are, of course, our responsibility.

Rachel Bolstad and Jane Gilbert

Introduction:
Senior secondary schooling and 21st century learning—issues and questions

The 20th century saw major changes to secondary education in New Zealand. In 1900 fewer than 10 percent of primary school graduates went to secondary school. Secondary schools charged fees and were designed to prepare students for university and the professions. Most of the population had little need for academic qualifications since it was easy to find employment where these were not required. However, as the country grew, so did the need for skilled tradespeople and administrators, and hence the need for more people with an education beyond the basics of primary school.

During the 1920s participation in secondary education increased rapidly.[1] This produced some challenges for the secondary schools of the time, which were not well set up to serve the needs of their

---

1 In 1900 the few students who went to secondary school came from families who could afford to pay the fees as, unlike primary education, secondary education was not yet free. The 1914 Education Act made state secondary education free to all those who had passed the primary school Proficiency Examination, and by 1917, 37 percent of primary school graduates went on to secondary school. After this, in the 1920s, uptake continued to increase rapidly.

new clientele. Following the English grammar school system they offered a traditional academic curriculum: subjects like mathematics and the sciences, English language and literature, Latin and other European languages, and history and geography. This curriculum was explicitly designed for students preparing for university study and was not especially suitable for those who were not.

Since the 1920s the junior secondary curriculum has undergone several major reforms designed to address the broader needs of a more heterogeneous secondary student population. However, nearly a century later the traditional academic curriculum continues to have a major influence on developments at the senior secondary level. Depending on one's point of view, this could be seen as a good thing or a bad thing. In this book we argue that it is time to take another look at some of the assumptions underpinning *both* points of view.

Now, in early 21st century New Zealand, nearly everyone goes to secondary school until at least Year 11, and more than half of all students go on to complete Year 13. Pressure from within—and outside—the education sector has produced major changes to the national qualifications system, which have often been controversial. Secondary school students can now study a plethora of new subjects, including media studies, dance, computer science, travel and tourism, enterprise studies, and outdoor education. The range of options available at the tertiary level is also now much greater, and the traditional divide between the academic, university-oriented pathway and the practical and/or vocationally oriented courses available at the former polytechnics is now blurred. These changes have been substantial, and have provided benefits for some. While they were probably necessary, in this book we argue that they are not sufficient as a framework for meeting the needs of 21st century New Zealand students. More thinking is needed.

At one level, the issues are similar to those faced in the 1920s (although the pressure points have shifted). However, on another level they are very different. The values, goals, and kinds of knowledge underpinning the traditional academic curriculum served the needs of a particular group of *people*. However—and this is important for our present purposes—they also served the needs of a particular moment in *time*, one we are no longer in.

This book takes a step back from current public discussions of what is happening in the upper levels of our secondary schools (much of which is focused on the merits and demerits of the National Certificate of Educational Achievement). Taking a big-picture look at where the current senior curriculum came from (and why), we argue that it is time to rethink many of its aims and objectives in the light of the—now very extensive—literature on the kinds of knowledge, skills, and dispositions people need to participate successfully in 21st century social and economic life. Our aim is to explore the big questions that education stakeholders—teachers, policy makers, parents, students, and employers—need to engage with as we redevelop the senior secondary curriculum for the 21st century. For example:

- What knowledge and skills do school leavers need to equip them for life in the 21st century? Are these different from what was needed in the past? If so, what is different? What should a 21st century New Zealand school graduate profile look like?
- Does our current senior secondary curriculum prepare young people for the variety of different postschool pathways that are now available?
- What kinds of people, with what kinds of skills, knowledge, and attributes, will we need to build and support a 21st century society and economy in New Zealand?
- Does the structure of our current senior secondary curriculum support our aspirations for New Zealand's future? If not, what might need to change?

However, before we can engage with these questions, which are about what sort of senior secondary curriculum we *should* have, we think it is first necessary to understand how and why we came to have the curriculum structures we have today. Part 1 of this book surveys the changing landscape of senior secondary education. It explores traditional and current aims and purposes, and looks at the opportunities—and the pitfalls—provided by the new environment. It then looks at the extent to which current aims and purposes fit with the demands of the globalised, knowledge-based societies of the future. Part 2 looks in detail at the structure of the current New Zealand senior secondary curriculum, exploring the complex mixture of ideas, contexts, and decisions that produced it. Finally, Part 3 explores some of the options for moving forward, looking at how we can preserve the best of what we have inherited from the past, while reconfiguring the system for 21st century needs.

We write this as researchers, as outsiders looking in on the policy process. One of us was once a secondary school teacher, but neither of us was involved in the educational policy, curriculum, or assessment developments we describe here. The development of the senior secondary curriculum (especially recently) has been an extremely complex process, and we think our outsider status made it easier for us not to get lost in the details (although at times this was difficult). Our goal has been to produce a big-picture conceptual analysis of the landscape, to lay out the issues we need to consider if we are to move ahead, and to explore these issues from the point of view of what is best for the learners—and for the society they will one day contribute to.

PART ONE

THE CHANGING LANDSCAPE OF SENIOR SECONDARY EDUCATION IN NEW ZEALAND

Introduction

Major curriculum change has been a feature of the New Zealand education landscape for many years. The last 15 to 20 years in particular have been a period of major review, refocusing, and revision. In 1993 the *New Zealand Curriculum Framework* was introduced. This set out the official school curriculum for Years 1 to 13 (that is, all of the years of schooling).[2] It was followed by a series of curriculum 'statements' for each of seven 'essential learning areas'.[3] In late 2006 a new draft national curriculum document was released and sent out for consultation,[4] and on 6 November 2007 the final version of *The New Zealand Curriculum for English-Medium Teaching and Learning in Years 1–13* was officially launched.[5] These documents represent the culmination of many years of research, review, consultation, and feedback. Since the Thomas Report in 1944,[6] the New Zealand school curriculum's aim has been to provide a coherent curriculum package that, because it is wide ranging, balanced, and based on a set of common goals for all learners, gives all students the basic platform of knowledge and skills they need to function in adult society.

While, in theory, the senior (that is, Years 11–13) school curriculum has been part of this ongoing review/revision process, in practice it hasn't. When students move out of Year 10 and into the upper secondary school, they move into an environment with an ethos and goals that are much more traditional. The junior secondary focus on a broad and balanced general education for all is replaced by a focus on more advanced and specialised forms of learning designed

---

2   Ministry of Education (1993).
3   These were: science; mathematics; English; arts; technology; social studies; and health and physical education.
4   Ministry of Education (2006b).
5   Ministry of Education (2007).
6   Department of Education (1944).

to prepare—and sort—students for a range of different postschool options. As a result, the discussions of the Years 11–13 curriculum have a different flavour from discussions of the Years 9 and 10 secondary curriculum.

Unlike the early secondary years curriculum, the senior curriculum is not a coherent package. It is made up of a series of discrete parts— the individual subjects that are taught in Years 11–13. Each of these subjects has its own independent set of goals and values and, in most cases, is derived from a body of knowledge that exists—and is developed and controlled—outside the school sector. Teachers of Years 11–13 students are subject specialists. They identify strongly with 'their' subject's knowledge and ways of doing things, and see their job as being to inculcate these things in their students. Teaching and learning are organised around the requirements of the subjects, on the one hand, and a high-stakes credentialing process on the other. Thus the shift to the senior curriculum involves a shift *away* from an approach that is, at least in theory, *learner* centred to one that is quite explicitly *knowledge* centred.

This subject-oriented focus is the product of a set of goals and values that have a long history. In this section we explore some of this history as a way of evaluating the extent to which it should continue to frame the shape and scope of student learning in the upper secondary school years. We then look at some of the pressures on the current curriculum, the reshaping of the curriculum–assessment relationship that has taken place since the 1990s, and the opportunities and possibilities that have been provided by this reshaping. Finally, we look at the work that is still needed if we are to provide young people with 21st century skills and knowledge, and evaluate the extent to which current curriculum and assessment practices are capable of doing this.

The traditional senior curriculum—where did it come from?

The traditional senior school curriculum is based on two important ideas:
(1) the importance of traditional disciplinary knowledge
(2) the need to sort people according to their likely employment destination.

These two ideas have very different origins, but were put together to build an education system that could serve the needs of an Industrial Age society.

The first idea can be traced back two and a half thousand years to the work of the Ancient Greek philosophers, in particular Plato and Socrates. Plato wrote a great deal about education. He set out a model for education that, he thought, would produce a stable, secure, and just society. His education system, while open to all, was specifically designed to produce the qualities needed in the 'philosopher kings'—or future rulers—of his ideal state. The curriculum of this system was explicitly *knowledge* centred. Plato thought that exposing individuals to *particular* kinds of knowledge—the best and greatest that human minds have been able to produce—would train their minds in ways that would allow their development to parallel the development of the best minds of the past. His model is the basis of the traditional academic curriculum in Western education systems.[7]

For most of the time since Plato, however, only a very small proportion of the population has had access to any form of education. Education for all, in Western countries, is a relatively recent phenomenon. It is only in the last 120 years or so that public, state-funded, compulsory schooling for *everyone* has been the norm. Two imperatives drove this development:
(1) the political philosophy of *egalitarianism* (the idea that everyone should have an equal chance to succeed in life)

---
7   Popper (1966).

(2) the *economic* need for people with the skills and dispositions necessary for work in the new Industrial Age enterprises.

Putting these two ideas together produces a powerful case for mass education. However, these ideas conflict in important ways. For one thing, everyone can't actually be equal, or even have an equal chance to succeed, in a highly segmented economy. This conflict is resolved through the use of a strategy which cleverly combines Plato's traditional academic curriculum with one of the Industrial Age's iconic concepts—the *production line*. Industrial Age education systems are organised, like production lines, to mass-produce standardised products.[8] Students are 'processed' through the system in 'batches', known as year groups or classes. A preset curriculum is 'delivered' to them in a preset order by people who specialise in different stages of the production. The tasks to be completed are broken down into bite-sized pieces. Students are guided through each stage in a way that allows them to gain certain specific skills ('the basics'), but which, ironically, often prevents them from 'thinking *between* the tasks',[9] and from seeing and understanding the big picture of what they are learning. As they pass through the system, students are subjected to various 'quality control' processes, designed to assess whether or not they 'measure up' to the system's standards. This one-size-fits-all, production-line approach is a very efficient way of dealing with large volumes of 'product'. It is also a reasonably efficient way of ensuring that most of the product meets certain basic standards, while at the same time allowing the system to sort out which of its products 'have what it takes' to go on for further processing.

In this system, the main instrument of quality control is the traditional academic curriculum. In the early 20th century the main

---

8 See, for example, Beare (2001); Beare & Slaughter (1993); Senge et al. (2000).
9 This idea comes from Skilton-Silvester (2003).

quality control points were at the primary–secondary transition (the Proficiency exam) and the early secondary years. Several attempts were made during the 20th century to broaden the focus of secondary education beyond the traditional academic subjects,[10] but the only substantive change has been to move the point at which these subjects are explicitly used to sort people to a higher level in the school system.

Why did things develop this way? How and why did the academic subjects come to have this function? Why are they seen as being more 'high value' than other subjects? How and why did the education system develop this sorting function? Asking and answering these questions is important because it allows us to examine how and why the current senior secondary curriculum has the structure it does, and to evaluate the extent to which this structure should continue to apply in the 21st century.

First of all, what is the basis of the idea that the traditional academic subjects are somehow better than the subjects with a more applied or practical orientation? Answering this involves a brief trip into the philosophy of knowledge and its history. Put simply, in the Western tradition there are two basic philosophies of knowledge. In one, known as rationalism, true knowledge is developed through thinking—not just any kind of thinking, but a particular, very deep kind of thinking that follows certain important rules (of logic and so on). In the other model, known as empiricism, knowledge is developed through experience and observation. These two approaches can be put together, and in some of the most powerful modern forms of knowledge—science, for example—they are. However, the rational (or thinking) part is usually the high-value part. This is because, although the thinking happens in the minds of

---

10 For example, the curriculum changes outlined above, but also the—largely unsuccessful—attempt in the 1920s and 1930s to establish a separate 'technical' high school system; see McKenzie (1992).

real people, because it follows certain important rules, this thinking is somehow *set apart* from people (their bodies, feelings, desires, and concerns): that is, it is *objective*. Knowledge that is produced from this kind of thinking is authoritative, rigorous, universal, timeless, and, above all, true. It is also often highly abstract and difficult. It involves brain work rather than manual work or work with the senses or emotions, and it involves following certain rules and procedures. Being able to produce this kind of knowledge requires a long apprenticeship. It requires many years of immersion in a discipline, supervised by expert practitioners.

Knowledge generated through experience and/or observation, on the other hand, has a lesser value (in the traditional scheme of things) because it *lacks* this objectivity. These forms of knowledge involve the body and the senses, and are often context dependent or situation specific. They are therefore *not* objective (or universal and timeless), and are less authoritative, less true. Thus one form of knowledge is high status because it *distances* itself from people, while the lower status of the other is because it *takes account of* people and context. This distinction is the basis of the academic–applied split in the school curriculum (and other contexts), and it is a distinction that is very deeply embedded in education's 'collective unconscious'.[11] Later (at the end of Part 1) we will argue that this distinction is no longer relevant in the 21st century. Next, however, we look at why we want our education system to be able to sort people.

As outlined earlier, Industrial Age education systems are premised on egalitarianism *and* the need to provide for the human resource needs of the economy. This is a bit of a problem. Industrial Age economies are highly stratified. Providing for the economy's human resource needs involves producing two broad classes of people—

---

11 By this we mean that this distinction is implicitly assumed, particularly by traditionalists, as being 'just how things are'. See Gilbert (2005), Chapters 2 and 6, especially pp. 159–161, for more on this argument.

those suited to the work involved in mass-producing the goods that are the source of economic wealth, and those who are more suited to management and/or professional roles. Egalitarianism, on the other hand, requires that everyone has an equal opportunity to succeed. This quandary is resolved by having an open-entry system that provides everyone with 'the basics' (and therefore an equal starting point), while rationing higher education to those who 'have what it takes' to benefit from it (a model characterised by former Director-General of Education Bill Renwick as 'bread for all and jam for the deserving').[12]

Underlying this approach are two important ideas. First is the idea that only a small proportion of the population really need the kinds of knowledge and skills developed in higher forms of education; second is the idea that the academic subjects that make up higher forms of education are a good preparation for a career in management or the professions. Among educationists, the first of these two ideas has long been questioned. We look at some of their arguments later. First, however, we want to look at the second assumption. Why do we believe that a curriculum that involves learning about calculus and algebra, about Shakespeare and Wordsworth, about the Krebs Cycle in respiration or the Second Law of Thermodynamics, is a good preparation for a career in management or the professions?

The first answer to this question takes us back to Plato. Learning this kind of knowledge, he would have argued, trains the mind. It builds the mind's capacity to think—and be organised—in certain highly specific ways. The second answer is that this kind of knowledge, for the reasons outlined earlier, is thought of as being high-quality knowledge, and students who are capable of learning it are therefore high-quality students. The ability to acquire this kind of knowledge can thus be used to decide who has what it takes for

---

12 Renwick (1986).

further study and who doesn't. Latin and the classics were once the key arbiters of ability, although in the last hundred years or so mathematics has taken over this role.

A third reason for using the traditional academic subjects for quality control is a little more prosaic. The *academic* reason for learning these subjects is to become part of one of the academic disciplines: it is how one is 'disciplined' into the discipline. This is a long process, involving learning to think and behave in certain ways, following certain rules, and respecting the authority of one's teachers. In most disciplines it involves developing the ability to think analytically—to break things down into parts, to examine them methodically and logically, in detail, in sequence, and usually out of context, to see how they are related.

These abilities and dispositions are required if one is to be an academic. However, they are also required in Industrial Age managers and professionals (although, unlike academics, these people do not really need a detailed understanding of the *knowledge* of these disciplines). A fourth reason, important from an educator's point of view, is that the knowledge that is the basis of the traditional academic subjects is knowledge that is easily organised into logical sequences of curriculum units that can be taught using expository, step-by-step methods, and assessed in ways that produce apparently clear, unambiguous results. This is important for fitting the egalitarian goal together with the sorting goal: the sorting systems have to be seen to be fair.

How is all this reflected in the New Zealand school curriculum? Figure 1 (see p. 20) is an attempt to show how the 'traditional' (that is, the pre-1990s) senior secondary curriculum functioned to mediate between the subject disciplines and the assessment system to sort people for the different postschool options.

Before major changes were made to New Zealand's qualification structures in the 1990s, there were three main sets of qualifications:

Figure 1 The traditional model for senior secondary curriculum (pre-1990s)[15]

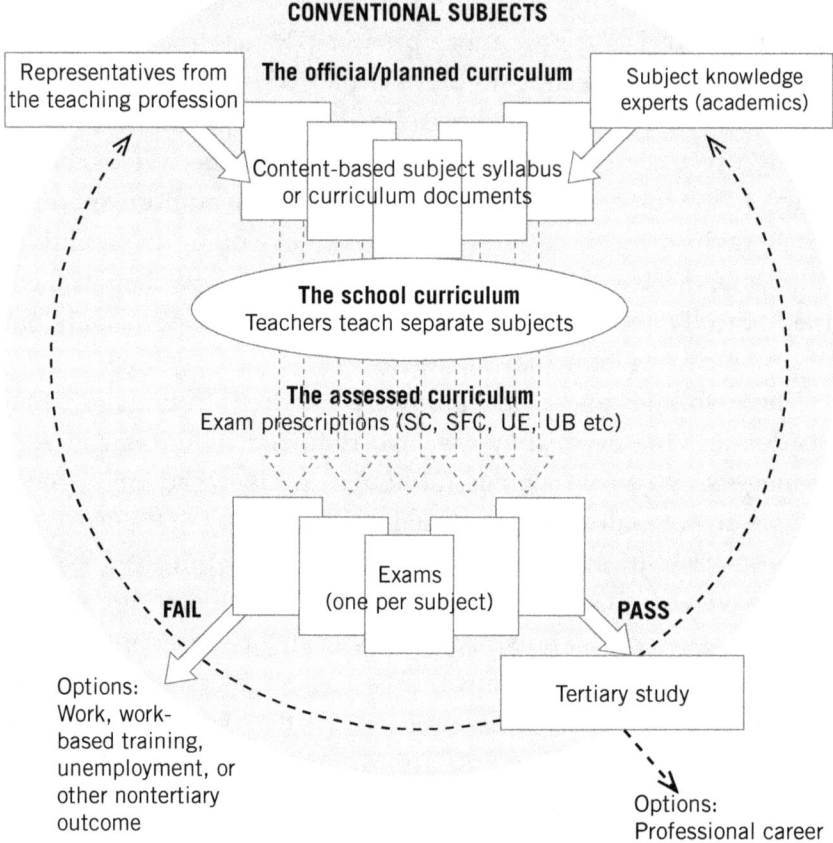

---

15 Note: SC is School Certificate; SFC is Sixth Form Certificate; UE is University Entrance; and UB is the University Bursaries examination.

(1) School Certificate, an examination students sat at the end of three years of secondary education (at the end of Form Five—now Year 11); (2) Sixth Form Certificate and University Entrance, at the end of four years of secondary education (Form Six—now Year 12); and (3) University Bursaries/Scholarships and Higher School Certificate, at the end of Form Seven—now Year 13.[13] Each of the subjects offered for these qualifications had its own syllabus and examination prescription. The syllabus documents were developed by subject-knowledge experts—usually academics—with representatives from the teaching profession. These documents were the *planned curriculum*. Teachers used these documents to produce the *school curriculum* (that is, the curriculum experienced by students), teaching subjects which corresponded in name and nature to the syllabus documents. The *assessed curriculum* was determined by the examination prescriptions, also developed by subject experts, which was, in theory, closely related to the *planned curriculum*. Students were assessed via external exams for each subject. If they passed, they were eligible to enter tertiary education (a university or a polytechnic). If they failed, they could get a job, enter work-based training, become unemployed, or take up some other nontertiary education option.

In this system the senior secondary curriculum is constructed in a top-down way that assumes—and is contained within—a particular model of knowledge (represented by the shaded area in Figure 1). The knowledge that is the basis of the curriculum comes from—and closely follows—the parent disciplines in the universities. Curriculum development was centrally controlled (by officials in the then Department of Education), and the subjects each had official national documents that outlined what students should be learning. Students were sorted for the various postschool options,

---

[13] In 1986 the university entrance part of this was moved into Form 7/Year 13 and made part of the University Bursaries examination.

and some would go on (as teachers or university academics) to later have an input into the maintenance and/or development of the curriculum.

This model was, for many years, stable and self-perpetuating. More recently, however, it has come under pressure. The relatively neat structure depicted in Figure 1 is being replaced by something that is much more complex and less coherent. We attempt to represent the new, messier structure in Figure 2 later (p. 42). First, however, we look at some of the developments that have put the traditional system under pressure.

New pressures and changes in the education landscape

The wider landscape into which senior secondary education must fit has changed in some important ways since the traditional model described above was developed. In the last 20 years or so the number of students staying on beyond the postcompulsory years has increased considerably. There has been major change in—and expansion of—the tertiary sector, and major changes to the school qualifications and assessment system. As a result, there is an increased emphasis on identifying and supporting different student pathways from school. In addition, the world beyond education has seen significant social, political, and economic change—change to which the education sector has not, as yet, been particularly responsive. These pressures are forcing new priorities and purposes on senior secondary education and calling into question many of the assumptions on which the traditional curriculum was based. This section looks at these pressures, under five general headings, and raises some questions for discussion.[14]

---

14 These questions appear in boxes at the end of each of the five sections. We don't suggest any answers: rather we think these questions need to be the focus of more general public discussion.

1. Increased retention rates

In the last couple of decades, most countries, for a variety of reasons, have experienced a marked increase in the number of students staying in school beyond the minimum school-leaving age.[16] In 1993 the New Zealand official school-leaving age (that is, the age at which it is no longer compulsory to be enrolled in a school) was increased from 15 to 16 years. This change was to be linked with the development of a raft of new 'transition' programmes designed to serve the needs of those who might otherwise have left at 15.[17]

As a result, today's secondary schools are required to cater for a large and diverse cohort of learners. Many of these learners have complex and varied curriculum needs, needs that most secondary schools are not particularly well set up to meet. Table 1 shows that the number of New Zealand students staying on at school until Year 13 more than doubled in the decade or so between the mid-1980s and the mid-1990s.

Table 1 Increase in retention rates (%) of New Zealand students, 1984–1995[18]

	1984	1995
Form 5/Year 11	86.8	97.0
Form 6/Year 12	56.7	80.5
Form 7/Year 13	18.3	48.3

Many of the students who stay on in school once it is no longer compulsory are there because they have been advised—by families, teachers, or others—that having a 'good' education will somehow

---

16 These reasons include 'credential inflation' (a pattern of continuous increase in the qualifications required for entry-level positions in most forms of work), and a greater expectation by the general public, supported by specific policies (including cuts to the youth unemployment benefit), that young people stay in school for longer.
17 See Ministry of Education (1992).
18 From Butterworth & Butterworth (1998).

result in a good job, or because they have no other options (because there are fewer jobs or job-related training programmes available to school leavers than was the case in the past). However, these students are often not especially interested in the subjects of the general academic curriculum, and if they don't have a clear reason for studying them, the ability of these subjects to meet their needs is questionable. It is not especially clear what a 'good' education would look like for these students, and we don't have an adequate framework for considering this question.

In addition, while overall retention rates are increasing, these increases do not apply equally to all groups. While there have been small improvements recently, the retention and achievement rates of Māori and Pasifika students, for example, are considerably lower than those of other groups. For example, in 1986 only 5 percent of Māori males and 5.7 percent of Māori females stayed at school until Form 7.[19] In 1997 the average length of stay at secondary school was 4.6 years for Pākehā students, 4.5 for Pasifika students, and only 4.1 for Māori students.[20] Moreover, in 1997, 38 percent of Māori students left school with no educational qualifications, compared with 26 percent of Pasifika students and 18 percent of all students.[21] By 2002, while 39 percent of Māori school leavers had at least Sixth Form Certificate, 35 percent left with no formal qualifications,[22] and in 2003, 30 percent of Māori were still leaving school with no qualifications.

Thus while, in general, a larger proportion of each year group is staying on the education production line for longer, Māori and Pasifika students are disproportionately represented among the system's rejects (or, looked at another way, those who have rejected

---

19 Royal Commission on Social Policy (1988).
20 Fiske & Ladd (2000).
21 *Ibid*.
22 Ministry of Education (2004).

the system). This has significant implications for New Zealand's future, given that, if current demographic projections are correct, over the next 50 years we will become a nation of predominantly Māori and Pasifika people.[23] If we do not find ways to address the cause of these groups' lower rates of participation and achievement, our overall levels of educational attainment will drop, and as a country we will be ill equipped to participate in the globalised world of the 21st century. The current one-size-fits-all system is clearly not meeting the needs of many students in this group. Many Māori and Pasifika students don't fit the system, and the system doesn't give them what they need to participate in 21st century life. Policy makers have developed a number of initiatives designed to 'close the gaps' between these different groups, but thus far these initiatives have largely focused on doing more of what we do now—or doing it better. We think something different is needed.

Questions

If the senior curriculum was originally designed to meet the needs of a small subset of the population (primarily those destined for university study), and it now has to meet the needs of just about everyone, then how much could—or should—it change?

Should the senior curriculum be more learner-centred? Could learning be more personalised? Or should students be given more support to succeed within the existing system? Should the system change to fit the students, or should students be given more help to fit the system?

Does the existing system prepare students well for life beyond school? Is that its purpose?

What would the benefits be if we changed the system? Would they be worth it?

---

23 See Cook (2000), or Ministry of Education (2000b) for summaries of these projections.

2. Expansion of the tertiary sector

Schooling has not been the only site of major change in the last two decades. The economic and social changes that produced higher retention rates in secondary schools during the 1980s and 1990s had a similar effect on the tertiary education sector.[24] Changing labour markets saw a decline in blue-collar jobs and an increase in white-collar jobs requiring higher skill levels and more education. Tertiary education was seen as more and more necessary to economic success. With more students staying in secondary school longer, there was a flow-on effect for tertiary learning. In the 16 years between 1985 and 2001 the number of New Zealand students in tertiary education doubled.[25]

Major reforms in the tertiary sector in this period produced a massive increase in the number of education providers, and there was a considerable increase in the range of options available to students.

> [Today's] tertiary-education sector is characterised by its diversity. It ranges from informal nonassessed community courses to four-year postgraduate degrees; from part-time self-paced learning courses studied extramurally or on the Internet, to courses involving full-time classroom-based tuition. It includes on-the-job training and apprenticeships, as well as adult and community education courses for people pursuing interests or hobbies and/or social interaction.[26]

As Table 2 shows, in 2005 most 16–17-year-olds were involved in full-time education,[27] but around 15 percent had left school and were enrolled in courses run by tertiary education providers.

---

24 McLaughlin (2003).
25 *Ibid*. For those in the traditional tertiary age group (between 18 and 24), participation went from 20.5 percent in 1990 to 34.8 percent in 2001. In 1999, 45.2 percent of school leavers went directly into tertiary education after leaving school.
26 Scott (2003), p. 10.
27 Sixteen years is currently the official school-leaving age—the age at which attendance at school is no longer compulsory. However, this age is currently under review and is likely to be raised.

Table 2 Participation rates in education for New Zealand students aged 16–19, 2005

Student age	16 % age group*	17 % age group	18 % age group	19 % age group
Schools	80	60	15	3
Tertiary education providers	14	15	39	45
Total participating in education	94	75	54	48

Source: Data provided by the Data Management and Analysis Division of the Ministry
of Education.
* Based on the total estimated June 2003 population of people in this age group.

The policy response to these developments has been to develop initiatives like the Secondary-Tertiary Alignment Resource (STAR), which aims to help senior secondary school students find suitable pathways into work or further study via work-based learning and/or tertiary-type study. According to the evaluators of STAR, this initiative:

> … provides a way for schools to acknowledge (and begin to deal with) the contestability of their school curriculum and pedagogy alongside those of universities, polytechnics, and other private tertiary establishments. In practice this opens up opportunities for school students to experience learning in different settings, trial their career aspirations, experience success in school, and gain credits towards qualifications which they can continue to pursue after leaving school.[28]

The evaluators found that STAR enabled schools to widen their curriculum, acknowledge the importance of vocational as well as academic learning, and re-engage students by presenting possible

---

28 Vaughan & Kenneally (2003), p. ix.

pathways to them. However, they also found that the tension between STAR's dual aims—to retain students *and* to assist them to leave school—left some STAR co-ordinators, school principals, and external providers confused about how to use STAR most effectively, and how best to realise its intent. This confusion was reportedly compounded by a lack of clear direction about which of these two aims, if either, should take greater priority.

Some communities have other initiatives for helping students to manage the transition from school. These nonschool-based programmes are funded in a variety of ways; for example, through the communities themselves, or youth organisations, or through Work and Income New Zealand.[29] Their aim—to reduce the large number of 15–19-year-olds in some communities who are 'dropping below the radar' (a group known officially as NEET, or Not in Education, Employment or Training)—and the necessity for their existence should alert us to the lack of fit between current education and training models and the realities of the labour market.

In the traditional secondary model, school leavers are supposed to be ready for further education or training, *or* for work. However, it is clear that the current senior school curriculum does *not* prepare a great many students for the realities of today's labour market. Few 16-year-olds will be able to go directly from school to work, yet the current funding models assume they can. Currently, 15–18-year-olds enrolled in schools have free places, but once they have left school they have to pay for places in tertiary courses (which, of course, means that many simply don't enrol). If schools are to fulfil the role of managing the school–work transition, they need to be equipped differently—with new and different curricula, and with teachers (and other staff) in new and different roles. The relationship between the secondary and tertiary sectors needs rethinking, and the concept of the school-leaving age needs re-evaluating.

---

29 For example, the COMET initiative in South Auckland.

> **Questions**
>
> What sort of relationship should there be between the secondary and tertiary sectors in the new environment? Which sector should take responsibility for helping and/or advising students as they manage the transition? Should schools be geared mainly towards preparing students for particular pathways (e.g., towards degree or diploma pathways)?
>
> Do students *need* to complete the traditional secondary school years before going on to tertiary courses? Is it just tradition (or funding arrangements) that constrain 15-year-olds from enrolling in tertiary courses? Should the boundaries between the two sectors be more permeable?
>
> Can we expect to see more 16- and 17-year-olds enrolling in tertiary programmes? What does this mean for secondary schools?
>
> Do we need new and different secondary school programmes for this age group?
>
> Or do we need to find ways to accommodate students who are learning in institutions other than secondary schools—or students who are learning in a number of different institutions at the same time?
>
> How should initiatives like STAR develop in the future? What should their priority be? What can we learn from them?

3. Changes to school qualifications and assessment systems

One result of the increasing diversity of the upper secondary school population, on the one hand, and recent changes to the tertiary sector, on the other, has been to produce a series of major changes to the school qualifications system. The official aim of these reforms has been to:

- accommodate the changing needs of an expanded postcompulsory student population
- expand the range of opportunities and pathways for 15–19-year-olds
- create clearer links and transitions between schooling, further education, vocational training, and the workforce
- support a 'lifelong learning' approach to formal education.

In 1990 the New Zealand Qualifications Authority (NZQA) was established and the National Qualifications Framework (NQF) was developed. The aim of the NQF was to support lifelong learning by making it easier for people to move freely between different parts of the education sector, receive appropriate recognition of prior learning, and access information about the full range of education options available:

> In the twenty-first century most people will undertake formal learning at a number of stages throughout their lives. Consequently, effective credit transfer systems will be increasingly important to enable people to return to learning at various stages in their lives so they can build on what they have previously achieved.[30]

Integral to the assessment and qualification changes of the 1990s was the move to standards-based assessment. The early reforms focused on developing Unit Standards and other qualifications for use in trade and technical qualifications. By 1993/94 the work on Unit Standards was widened to include school subjects and other learning areas. By the end of the 1990s the NQF was set to recognise and facilitate transferability of learning and credits/qualifications at eight levels, from School Certificate (NQF Level 1) through to postgraduate tertiary study (NQF Level 8). Then, towards the end of 1998, it was announced that a new, unified system of qualifications would be introduced for all New Zealand senior secondary students: the National Certificate of Educational Achievement (NCEA). The NCEA was to be the main qualification for 16–19-year-olds. Its aim was to recognise a wide range of learning, in senior secondary school and beyond school. This restructuring of the school qualifications system was controversial and resisted by many inside and outside the education sector.

The government's main aim during the 1990s was to develop a 21st century assessment and qualifications system. Debate among educationists focused on how to assess, what to assess, and

---

30 New Zealand Government (1999).

what kinds of assessment tools were appropriate for the various qualifications. There was no official parallel discussion of what a 21st century *curriculum* for senior secondary students might look like, and recent research shows that the opportunities for curriculum change that are, in theory, provided by the NCEA system of assessment have not yet been taken up. In particular, the content and teaching of the traditional academic subjects has changed very little.[31]

This was, at least in part, a consequence of the processes that were used to develop the new assessment system. Once the NCEA was recognised as the main school qualification, many of the subject areas began to develop Achievement Standards.[32] In most cases this was done by teacher groups using their subject's existing curriculum 'statement'. These statements, developed in the 1990s to replace the old syllabus and examination prescription documents, were supposed to complement the National Curriculum Framework. In practice, in some subject areas they were used *instead* of the National Curriculum Framework. Where there were no already-existing curriculum statements (in the cases of many of the locally developed, emerging, or explicitly vocational subjects), a miscellany of other non-nationally mandated documents, including course prescriptions and outlines, were used to develop Achievement Standards. While the National Curriculum Framework (and the new *New Zealand Curriculum* (2007)) officially sets 'the direction for learning for all students while at school' (i.e., up until Year 13), it is compulsory for schools to follow only until Year 10. In theory, the school curriculum is seamless from Years 1–13, but in practice there is a sharp disjuncture between Years 10 and 11, when Achievement Standards and/or Unit Standards become the *de facto* curriculum.

---

31 These findings come from the Learning Curves research project (Hipkins & Vaughan, 2002; Hipkins, Vaughan, Beals, & Ferral, 2004).
32 Achievement Standards are the new standards-based qualification units that students now aim to achieve. Achievement Standards in some curriculum areas replaced the early Unit Standards, although most of the specifically vocationally oriented areas kept Unit Standards.

This situation does not appear to have been explicitly planned, but to have evolved out of the recent changes. The decision to make the National Curriculum Framework noncompulsory after Year 10 was probably an artefact of the assumptions that underpin the traditional model. As outlined earlier, it was at this point that the traditional senior secondary curriculum (and its purposes) were clearly separated from the early secondary years. The series of assumptions that underpinned this decision probably need re-evaluating in the present context.

> **Questions**
>
> To what extent have traditional ideas about the purpose of assessment in secondary schools (sorting, rationing, ability, and so on) influenced—and possibly confounded—the attempt to develop a 21st century qualifications system?
>
> How did it come about that we focused on the assessment and qualifications system first? That is, why did we focus on how to measure what has been learnt before debating the question of what students might need to learn in the 21st century? Or the question of how they might best be helped to learn it?
>
> Why is it that, despite the changes to the assessment system, the traditional split between the academic and the applied subjects is still there? Why is it that the traditional academic subjects are still taught in much the same ways as they always were?
>
> Why has there not yet been a debate about how and why the senior school curriculum should be different in the 21st century?

4. Emphasis on student 'pathways' and 'transitions' from school

The changes outlined above have led to new ways of thinking about—and representing—how students might make the transition from school to work or tertiary education. It is now common to see the 'pathways' metaphor used in this context, and the meaning of the term 'transition' has changed. In the past there was really only one recognised successful pathway from senior secondary school: the academic pathway to higher education. The term 'transition', meaning transition to work, represented a kind of failure, and was the poor cousin of academic achievement.[33] Transition was the name given to the programmes offered to students who were not achieving academically. These programmes aimed to give students work skills and/or work experience before leaving school, often to take up semiskilled or unskilled work.

The pathways metaphor is meant to signal a new view, one that acknowledges that there are many different and valid routes and destinations available to senior secondary learners, including, but not limited to, the academic pathway to tertiary studies. The term 'pathways' also implies seamlessness: the notion that people will experience progression and continuity between educational institutions, between education or training courses, and between careers.[34] Thus transition is now something that is important for *all* students, not just those *not* pursuing an academic school-to-tertiary pathway.

The pathways metaphor also represents a new way of thinking about how schools should support their senior students. Underpinning it is the idea of empowering students to map their own pathway, and to be actively involved in making decisions and choices about their school subjects, their overall school programme, future plans they may have, and institutions they might attend.[35] Schools have come under pressure to reorganise the senior curriculum so that it provides better 'sign posts' for students as they make the transition to postschool settings.[36] However, currently there is little support for schools to do this in ways that fit with existing practices. The new emphasis on student pathways and/or transition from school has been tacked on to the traditional system which, as we have seen, was set up for other, quite different purposes. Requiring schools to actively support students as they transition out of school is a change

---

33 Vaughan (2003).
34 *Ibid.*
35 Brewerton (2004).
36 Dwyer (1995), p. 147.

to schools' traditional function. If it is to be done well, this requires some rethinking—and reprioritising—of our ideas about schooling's purposes at this level.[37]

New Zealand schools are required to provide career guidance for all students in Year 7 and above.[38] Career guidance in 21st century schools involves far more than choosing a suitable career. It involves helping students navigate the plethora of different pathways available to them by providing information, training courses, counselling, and so on. Many schools have extensive systems and huge databases on the pathways and career options available to students.[39] Recent New Zealand research shows that many schools are providing multiple course options *within* core subjects like English and mathematics in Years 11–13.[40] The development of these different course options is based on the premise that students have different needs, interests, and abilities, and different learning pathways, and that courses should be tailored to reflect these. Choosing which course option to take requires good information and support for students about the differences between these courses, and the consequences of taking various courses in terms of the pathways they open up or close off as students progress to their next year of learning.[41]

However, simply adding the pathways metaphor to the existing framework is likely to subvert its intended meaning. In an Industrial Age education system, the pathways metaphor brings to mind other, not especially empowering, metaphors. For example, pathways implies channelling, directing, moving along a trajectory, and/or moving from one point to another in a unidirectional and orderly way. It also implies choices—choosing one pathway over another—as well as the idea that pathways lead to something, as opposed to

---

37 *Ibid.*
38 Under the National Administration Guidelines.
39 Vaughan (2003), pp. 1–14.
40 Hipkins et al. (2004).
41 Brewerton (2004).

something *else*, and that the journey is linear, step-by-step and predictable.[42] These ideas are characteristic of Industrial Age thinking and, in this context, are probably a reasonably fair and efficient way of organising things. However, if our focus is on preparing students for life and work in the 21st century, then these ideas need rethinking. We cannot assume a known future, a known set of options to choose between, each requiring a known set of knowledge, skills, and aptitudes, and therefore a known—and well-trodden—pathway.[43] We need some new metaphors, some new ways of thinking about what is—or, more importantly, should be—going on here if we are to build a 21st century senior secondary schooling system. Part 3 of this book looks at how we might begin to develop these. In the next section, however, we explore how and why a 21st century curriculum needs to be different from a 20th century one.

> **Questions**
>
> With so many more options available to students than in the past, how well equipped are secondary schools to provide the necessary levels of advice and guidance to today's senior secondary learners?
>
> To what degree should the senior secondary curriculum be geared towards a pathways approach?
>
> Should the curriculum be structured to support students to specialise their learning for a particular pathway, or should it try to ensure that students have breadth, balance, and common learning experiences?
>
> Is it the school's role to channel and help students into particular pathways?

5. The Knowledge Society and 21st century learning

As we have seen, by the end of the 20th century the idea that *all* students need the full 4–5-year package of secondary education was widely accepted. The related idea, widely held among educationists,

---

42 Vaughan (2003); Vaughan & Boyd (2005); Vaughan, Roberts, & Gardiner (2006).
43 See p. 15 above.

that *all* students—not just those who fit easily into the present system—need the knowledge and skills traditionally delivered only in higher education has emerged out of the Knowledge Society literature. This literature tells us that, socially, politically, and economically we have moved out of the Industrial Age into the Knowledge Age (or, for some authors, the Conceptual Age), and that as a result, many of our traditional institutions need rethinking.[44]

Knowledge Age economies rely not on extracting natural resources for use in manufacturing, but on *ideas*. However, knowledge in this context does *not* mean 'stuff' that people 'get' and store away. It has a new meaning, one that differs in major ways from the one that underpins our education system. Knowledge, in the Knowledge Age, *does* things; it makes things *happen*. As one commentator puts it, knowledge is no longer thought of as if it were a kind of matter: instead it is seen as being more like energy.[45] It is no longer something produced by expert individuals (academics, or scientists, for example); rather, it is something that happens in teams—in the connections and relationships between people, and between people and ideas. It is a process, not a product, and is no longer universal and timeless, but constantly evolving, flowing, and regenerating into new forms.

These ideas come from research that followed the cultural shifts in thousands of business and government organisations in North America and Western Europe during the 1980s and 1990s (changes that, it has to be assumed, have similarly affected other Western countries); that is, in the kinds of organisations that a great many of the young people now in secondary school can expect to work in. The literature based on this research does *not* claim that the mass-production of goods has ceased, or that there are no longer jobs for

---

44 For a fuller description of this literature and its implications for education, see Gilbert (2005), especially Chapters 2 and 6.
45 Castells (2000).

traditional academics. However, it does draw our attention to the fact that most mass-production jobs (and, increasingly, many aspects of professional jobs)[46] are now being outsourced to cheaper parts of the world, and to the impact of recent restructuring in the government-funded research sector on the work of academics, scientists, and other researchers.

All this has obvious implications for the traditional senior school curriculum. As we saw earlier, the current education system is an Industrial Age system. It is designed to sort people according to their suitability for two broad classes of Industrial Age jobs: those requiring physical strength, manual dexterity, respect for authority, and the ability to follow instructions; and those requiring logical, analytical thinking and attention to detail, as well as respect for authority and the ability to follow rules. If we accept what the Knowledge Age literature has to say, *neither* of these two broad classes of people will be needed in the future. While some of these attributes will be needed in a few people, most people will need much *more* than this.

These predictions are being acknowledged in current policy work, but in the educational context the response so far has been to focus on strategies designed to develop certain important skills (learning skills, creativity, ingenuity, and the ability to innovate, for example) and 'competencies'.[47] Current debate is focused on how best to develop these skills (or competencies), and how to assess the extent to which they have been developed (questions that, in Industrial Age educational thinking, are very difficult to answer). While these things are important, they gloss over *the* key message of the Knowledge Society literature: the change in knowledge's

---

46 See, for example, Thomas Friedman's (2006) book *The World Is Flat: A Brief History of the Twenty-First Century*.
47 The new curriculum for Years 1–13 emphasises the development of five key competencies: thinking; using language, symbols, and texts; managing self; relating to others; participating and contributing.

meaning, and the implications this has for the subject matter of the school curriculum and our orientation to it.

If the senior school curriculum is to be a useful preparation for life in the Knowledge Age, it needs to take account of this new view of knowledge. It needs to be based on a view of knowledge as being more like a verb than a noun, as a resource to do things with, not an object to be mastered. Instead of tasks and activities designed to reproduce existing knowledge, students need activities designed to allow them to work with knowledge to generate new knowledge. As Chris Bigum argues, we need to start seeing our schools as sites of knowledge *production*, not knowledge consumption.[48] Or, as Carl Bereiter puts it, we need to restructure school activities to resemble the working of research groups, groups engaged in collaborative new knowledge building designed to solve real-world problems. Schools, Bereiter says, are not research organisations, and nor are they miniature enterprises. They are more like miniature societies, and because of this we should reconfigure them as 'laboratories for testing designs for the Knowledge Age'.[49]

Bigum and Bereiter use the knowledge-creation concept to mean something much more than learning, in the sense in which this term is used in schools. The knowledge they are talking about is not an already-existing thing that can be acquired and stored away in someone's mind for future use. It is something completely new, something that, while it can contribute to an individual's learning, also contributes to world knowledge. This knowledge creation doesn't take place just in the minds of individuals, but in the relationships and connections *between* people, between people and ideas, and between people and existing knowledge.

It is for this reason that, despite the claims made by some commentators, the traditional forms of knowledge still matter.

---

48 Bigum (2003)
49 Bereiter (2002). The quote is from p. 462.

However, the *reasons* they matter are now very different. In a 21st century curriculum, knowledge can no longer be seen as a static end in itself (and the teacher's job done when students can reproduce it). Rather, traditional knowledge is the raw material for the kind of knowledge creation described above. It is a resource for what the French philosopher of knowledge Jean-François Lyotard calls 'performativity': the ability to take elements from one (old) knowledge system and put them together with elements from another to make *new* knowledge.[50] If they are to do this, learners will of course need to know quite a lot about how a number of different old knowledge systems work (i.e., they need to know something about how scientists, historians, mathematicians, and/or literary critics work, and how they go about creating new knowledge in their disciplines). They also need good skills in mediating, translating, and moving between the different disciplines. In the Knowledge Age, this kind of systems or metalevel knowledge and the ability to move between disciplines is more important than just knowing the detailed facts of those disciplines. Thus 21st century learners need to be able to do more than just *reproduce* knowledge. They must be able to actively *interact with* it: to understand, critique, manipulate, create, and transform it.

Working with knowledge to generate new knowledge requires different kinds of thinking from those emphasised in Industrial Age contexts. While the left-brain—systematic, logical, sequential, and detail-focused—thinking that was important for success in the Industrial Age is still necessary, it is, the futures literature tells us, *no longer sufficient*. According to Daniel Pink, for example, in what he calls the new Conceptual Age, 'big picture' thinkers, 'pattern recognisers', and 'meaning makers' will, as he puts it, 'rule the future'. He argues that, in this new age, the individuals and

---

50 Lyotard (1984).

organisations that will survive and prosper will be those with the ability to create products and services that people want (in an age of over-abundance) *and* that can't be produced more cheaply or faster by overseas knowledge workers (or machines). Pink summarises this set of skills in the phrase 'high concept/high touch'. 'High concept' for him 'involves the ability to create artistic and emotional beauty, to detect patterns and opportunities, to craft a satisfying narrative, and to combine seemingly unrelated ideas into a novel invention'. 'High touch', on the other hand, 'involves the ability to empathize, to understand the subtleties of human interaction, to find joy in one's self and elicit it in others, and to stretch beyond the quotidian, in pursuit of purpose and meaning.'[51]

Pink says that the high-value people will be the creators and empathisers. Right-brain—metaphorical, contextual, simultaneous, aesthetic—thinking will be valued over left-brain thinking, as will the ability to understand, interpret, synthesise and personalise products and services for the particular needs of individual consumers.

This view of knowledge—and thinking—differs in major ways from the one emphasised in today's education system. Redeveloping our education system for the Knowledge Age involves far more than aiming to produce more people with more of the *same* kinds of knowledge as was emphasised in the past. It requires a substantial rethinking of the curriculum and the assumptions that underpin it.

---

51 Pink (2006), pp. 51–52.

> **Questions**
>
> What would a senior secondary curriculum designed to prepare students for a successful and productive life in the Knowledge Age look like?
>
> What kinds of knowledge and attributes might students need in the jobs of the future, and is the curriculum we have now well suited to helping students develop these?
>
> To what extent does the current senior secondary curriculum's emphasis on the subject matter of 'old' knowledge need to be rethought?
>
> How can the dispositions and skills outlined above be taught? Is this the role of the senior secondary school?
>
> How can these dispositions, skills, and orientations to knowledge be assessed? How will we know if/when learners have developed them?
>
> What are the implications of all this for the traditional secondary school qualifications system? For our desire to sort people? For the relationship between the secondary and tertiary sectors?
>
> Does the current focus on channelling students into appropriate pathways reflect old (i.e., Industrial Age) assumptions about economic stratification? Given what the literature has to say on 21st century skills and dispositions, should we not be discussing how we can ensure that *all* students leave school with these skills and dispositions?

The senior secondary school today—education for the 21st century?

The changes outlined in the previous section have challenged—and continue to challenge—the traditional secondary system in major ways. When compared to the traditional model depicted in Figure 1 (p. 22 above), today's senior secondary curriculum looks complicated and very messy. Figure 2 below is an attempt to represent the current curriculum visually.

Some elements of the traditional model are still clearly visible (represented by the dark grey field). However, today's curriculum has had many new influences added to it. One major new influence is the idea of lifelong learning (represented by the light grey field); that is, the expectation that people will move between different work and education settings throughout their lives. This idea is supported by a

Figure 2 A picture of the senior secondary curriculum today

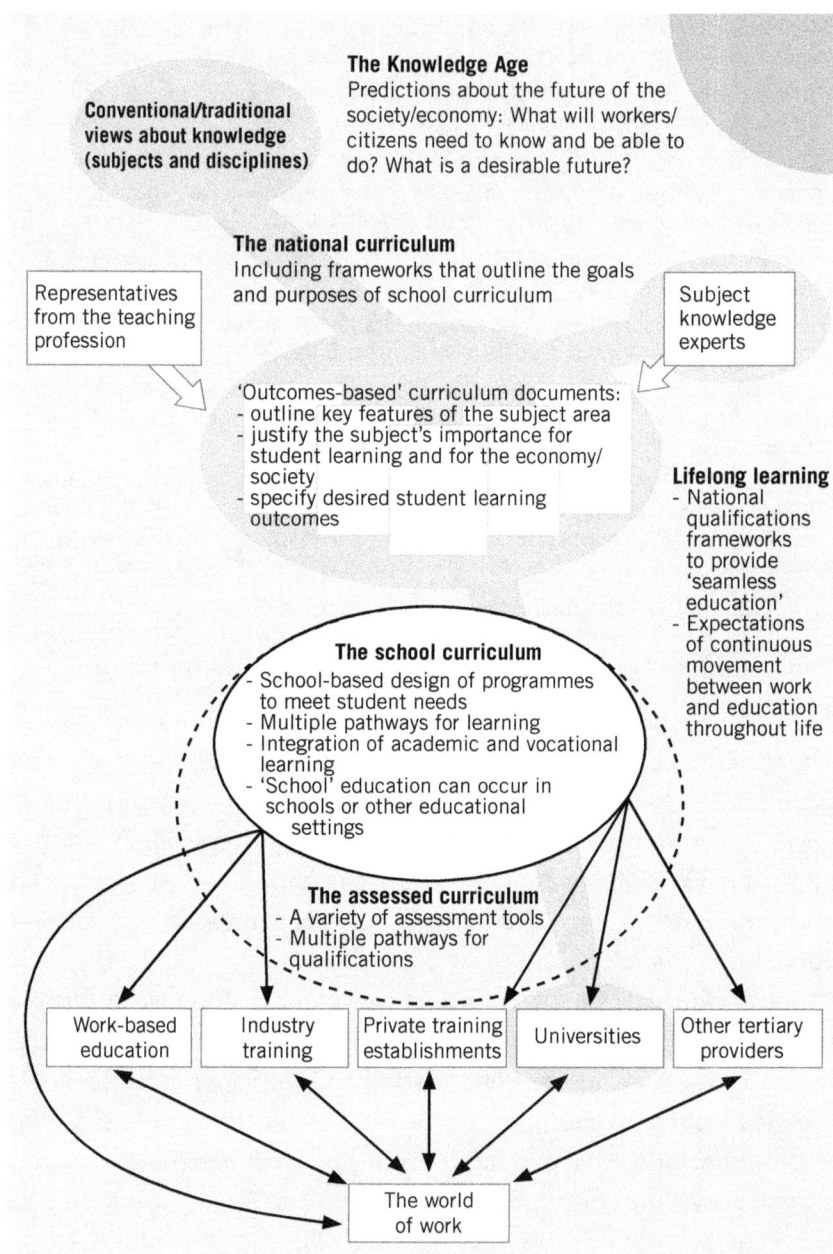

national qualifications framework that allows multiple qualification pathways for senior secondary and tertiary students. Thus there is no longer a direct relationship between the planned curriculum and the assessed curriculum as there was in the traditional model (that is, one exam prescription for each subject, derived from the contents of the curriculum/syllabus document). Instead, schools can choose from a variety of different assessment tools, and offer students a range of qualifications.

Another key new influence is that critical curriculum and assessment decisions are now made at the school level, decisions that have a significant influence on the experiences, opportunities, and forms of accreditation available to students.

The 1990s reforms to the old zoning system produced an environment which encouraged schools to compete with one another, often reconfiguring themselves for niche markets. Some, usually in areas with low retention rates or poor senior secondary student achievement, developed alternative or nontraditional learning pathways,[52] while others made the decision to offer curricula and assessment systems developed in other countries (the International Baccalaureate or the Cambridge examination system, for example).

In addition, new stakeholders have entered the picture, competing with the universities' traditionally strong influence on the shape and content of the curriculum. Some—including employer groups and industry representatives—are contributing to the development of Unit Standards, particularly in service and industry-related areas like the food and hospitality, manufacturing, and engineering and technology sectors.

All this is further complicated by the influence of the future-focused thinking discussed above. These ideas are shown at the top right-hand side of the diagram as a ripple. The result of all this

---

52 Boyd, McDowall, & Cooper (2002).

is that today's secondary school curriculum is significantly more complex, messier, and more contested than the traditional model. These new influences raise a number of questions, many of which will be very difficult to address from within the context of the traditional framework.

Our answers to the questions we have raised depend, to a large extent, on what we think a curriculum *is*.[53] If we see the curriculum as mainly an information-transmitting device—that is, as a coherent set of things-to-be-learnt—then decision making will mainly involve deciding which knowledge is most important. But important to—or for—whom? Academics? Teachers? Employer or industry groups? Parent/whānau or community groups? In the past, the answers to these questions seemed clearer, largely because senior secondary education had a more limited focus. Today, however, we have no framework, no starting point for considering these questions. Answering them will be extremely difficult, and in the present context the solutions we come up with are likely to be the result, not of principled debate, but of political compromise.

Alternatively, we could see the curriculum as a tool for shaping individual, group, and national identity. If this is its purpose, then we need to consider questions such as: What kind of people do we want to be? What kind of community do we want? What form of schooling could help us be those kinds of people and have that kind of community? Considering these questions obviously requires input from many people with many different interests. How should we go about balancing these different interests? Again, in the past this seemed clearer. Certain political ideals predominated and some groups had more influence than others on these debates. If curriculum development takes place at the local—or school—level to meet local needs, then students in different areas will obviously

---

53 Reid (1987).

learn different things. This of course raises the question of whether or not this will result in some students being disadvantaged.

> **Questions**
>
> If the contribution of employer groups and industry representatives to curriculum development is now seen as legitimate and reasonable, what about the nonservice and industry areas? For example, should employers and industries in the IT, finance, or film/media sectors be asked to contribute to the senior school curriculum's construction?
>
> Could students benefit from closer relationships between schools and businesses, or other groups in the community?
>
> Can such groups play a role in curriculum development without reconstituting secondary education as pre-employment training? Does pre-employment training belong in the school sector?
>
> What role should parents, whānau, and/or local communities play in developing the senior school curriculum? What about the schools themselves and the boards of trustees? Should senior curriculum be centrally developed and standardised, or locally developed for local conditions?
>
> What does a 'successful school leaver' look like in the 21st century?
>
> What will the workplaces of the future need from the school leavers of the future?
>
> Where do young people learn the things that make them successful in school and beyond school? What is the shape of the 'portfolio' of learning needed by young people at school?
>
> Should these questions be decided centrally or locally? Should schools and their communities help shape the postcompulsory school curriculum? How can schools achieve an appropriate balance between local interests and national interests, personal interests and wider social interests, and so on?
>
> How much diversity could, or should, there be between the curriculum offered in different schools?
>
> To what extent could school-based curriculum development in the senior school create disparities in the opportunities and postschool pathways available to students in different parts of the country?

The input of new, nontraditional influences has muddied the waters of the traditional model, summarised in Figure 1 above. Today's curriculum is underpinned by at least two quite different epistemologies, or models of what counts as knowledge[54] (and, as a result, two different assessment regimes), and at least two different understandings of the learner–worker identity that is to be developed.[55]

This, philosophically speaking, is a problem. While it is not a new one, it is a problem that the advent of the Knowledge Age forces us to address. The question of what kinds of knowledge matter in education, and the related one of what kinds of learner–citizen–workers the public education system should develop, have long been debated. However, they have not been resolved, largely because educational thinking in this area is rather muddled. We do not have a single coherent theory of knowledge: we do not have an agreed way of deciding what we think knowledge *is*, what good knowledge is (that is, valuable, useful, robust, or productive knowledge), or what forms of knowledge people need to know. In educational thinking, it is common to assume that knowledge is a key tool for producing the kind of society we want. But what kinds of knowledge, and what kinds of society? Emphasising one kind of knowledge over another means that we will produce—or reproduce—a certain kind of society. We have needed better theories of knowledge for a long time, but as we try to reconfigure our education system for the Knowledge Society the need is even more pressing. We need a theory that can allow for different forms of knowledge, while at the same time having a way of deciding what knowledge is good knowledge, and what knowledge isn't.[56]

Part 3 of this book returns to the question of what a curriculum is—or should be. We think that we are at an important moment in

---

54 See p. 15 above.
55 See the following for empirical work that documents and analyses this trend: Boreham (2002); Shacklock, Hattam, & Smyth (2000); Tennant & Yates (2005); Yates (2006).
56 For a more detailed discussion of these issues, see Chapter 6 of Gilbert (2005).

this country's educational history. We are just beginning the process of seriously engaging with the question of how best to provide the kinds of education needed for life and work in the 21st century. A number of different options for the way forward are in front of us.[57] Part 3 reviews some of these options. However, before considering which of these options is most appropriate, we first need to look in a little more detail at exactly how the ideas discussed here have played out in the construction of the current official New Zealand secondary curriculum. This is the purpose of Part 2.

---

57 See, for example, the work of the Secondary Futures project (www.secondaryfutures.co.nz), the *Students First* paper that is part of this work (Durie, 2006), as well as Brewerton (2004); Growth and Innovation Advisory Board (2005).

PART TWO

THE SENIOR CURRICULUM IN NEW ZEALAND TODAY—FRAMEWORKS, STRUCTURES, AND STANDARDS

In Part 1 we looked at the New Zealand senior secondary curriculum at the big-picture level, at the influences and pressures that are challenging the traditional approach to school learning at this level. In this section, we look at the structures and frameworks that underpin today's curriculum and explore some of the decisions that were made as these systems evolved in response to the changing environment. The story of the development of today's senior secondary curriculum is surprisingly complicated. Assembling it was a bit like assembling a jigsaw, and we found it difficult not to get lost in the details. Our aim was to try to see the senior secondary curriculum as a whole, to look at—and evaluate—its recent development in terms of its ability to produce 21st century learners.

In the first section of Part 2 we outline the regulatory frameworks governing the New Zealand school curriculum. We then look at the reforms that have affected senior secondary curriculum, assessment, and qualifications between the late 1980s and today, at three levels—the *national curriculum* (the official curriculum documents that set the overall direction of learning); the *school curriculum* (the teaching and learning experienced by students); and the *assessed curriculum* (the learning assessed by the various qualification systems)—and explore the interactions between these three levels.

The regulatory frameworks for the New Zealand Curriculum

The last 20 years or so have seen major reforms of the administration of New Zealand schools. These reforms have changed school practices, including curriculum and assessment, in significant ways. Beginning in 1989, the reforms now known as *Tomorrow's Schools* decentralised school governance and management to individual schools via boards of trustees.[58] Schools became responsible for implementing various legal requirements through the National Education Guidelines (NEGs) and the National Administration

---

58 Department of Education (1988).

Guidelines (NAGs). The curriculum responsibilities of schools are set out in the National Administration Guidelines. NAG 1 states that:

> Each Board of Trustees is required to foster student achievement by providing teaching and learning programmes which incorporate the New Zealand Curriculum (essential learning areas, essential skills and attitudes and values) as expressed in National Curriculum Statements.[59]

In the early 1990s, a national curriculum framework for all levels (Years 1–13) of all New Zealand schools was developed and mandated. However, as we argue below, the effects of other developments, combined with the influence of past approaches to schooling in the senior secondary years, have meant that the *New Zealand Curriculum Framework* (NZCF) did not, in practice, set the direction for learning in Years 11–13. Why is this? Does it matter? To answer these questions, we need to look back at the previous system.

The pre-1990s senior secondary curriculum

As outlined in Part 1 of this book, before 2002 the New Zealand senior secondary school curriculum had close links with the three main qualifications: School Certificate, Sixth Form Certificate, and University Bursary. Most of the senior subjects (mathematics, economics, English, history, geography, health, art, physical education, and other languages) had syllabus documents that were, in effect, the curriculum.[60] However, not all did: for example, there was no syllabus for senior science,[61] and the content of the specialist science subjects (chemistry, biology, and physics) was

---

59 Ministry of Education website www.minedu.govt.nz
60 Published and distributed by the Department, later Ministry, of Education.
61 The science syllabus before the NZCF applied only to Forms 1–5. A new Forms 1–4 science document was being developed, but with the introduction of the NZCF this was shelved (Bell, Jones, & Carr, 1995).

largely driven by the examination prescriptions. Before 1993 the senior science 'curriculum' consisted of a collection of nine examination prescriptions with no curriculum statement to link them.[62] For these subjects the examination prescriptions were the *de facto* curriculum.

Before the 1990s curriculum development involved producing subject syllabus documents, course statements, and/or examination prescriptions, and it was a centrally controlled process. School Certificate was controlled by the Department of Education, and from time to time curriculum committees were formed to develop School Certificate prescriptions. University Entrance, University Scholarship, and University Bursary were controlled by the University Entrance Board. This board had a subject committee for each subject, which developed and revised the University Entrance or University Bursary course prescriptions as needed. From time to time, new subjects were developed, usually in response to pressure from groups of teachers and/or university academics; for example, the emergence of media studies in secondary schools in the early 1980s,[63] or the introduction of physical education as a University Bursary subject. If they gained central approval from the Department of Education or the University Entrance Board, these subjects could become nationally recognised as official School Certificate, Sixth Form Certificate, or University Bursary subjects. At sixth form level, in addition to teaching nationally recognised Sixth Form Certificate subjects, schools could also develop 'local' subjects.

The introduction of the 1990s New Zealand Curriculum

In the 1990s work began on the documents that would make up the new national curriculum. The first three national curriculum statements (mathematics, English, and science) were gazetted early

---

62 Bell et al. (1995), p. 34.
63 See, for example, Horrocks & Hoben (2005).

in the 1990s and the old syllabus documents were revoked. By 2001 most of the new curriculum documents associated with the current national curriculum had been published, superseding the old subject syllabus statements. The extent to which these new documents influenced the *school* curriculum and the *assessed* curriculum at upper secondary level was, however, variable. In the 2001 *School Qualification Handbook*, some course statements and examination prescriptions referred to a national curriculum statement (e.g., *English in the New Zealand Curriculum*, *Mathematics in the New Zealand Curriculum*, *Physics in the New Zealand Curriculum*, *Japanese in the New Zealand Curriculum*). Others referred to earlier Department of Education syllabuses or draft syllabuses (e.g., *Economics Syllabus Forms 3 to 7*, *Draft Text and Information Management Curriculum*). One subject (accounting) referred to a document produced by the New Zealand Commerce and Economics Teachers' Association (*NZCETA Accounting Curriculum Statement for New Zealand Schools*), and many course prescriptions did not refer to any syllabus or curriculum document.

Thus the relationship between the new official national curriculum and the *de facto* senior secondary curriculum was unclear and inconsistent for most of the 1990s. The *School Qualifications Handbook* provided annual course statements and prescriptions for nationally approved senior secondary curriculum subjects, stating exactly what students needed to know and be able to do in those subjects to be prepared for their examinations and internal assessments, and while the old examination system remained in place it was, it appears business as usual.

The introduction of NCEA

In the late 1990s, after many years of pressure from the education sector, the old norm-referenced examination-based system of assessment was largely phased out. School Certificate, Sixth Form Certificate, and University Bursary examinations were replaced by a new, three-level qualification system called the National Certificate of Educational Achievement, or NCEA.

In the old external-examination-based system students were given percentage marks, which were derived by ranking them in relation to all other students in their year group for that subject. In this system, known as 'norm-referencing', the raw marks generated by students, usually in a three-hour exam, are scaled to produce a normal curve. The percentage mark a student is given depends on their place on that curve. An allocated mark (or agreed value) of 50 percent or higher is a pass, while a mark lower than 50 percent is a fail. For most of the 20th century the system was designed so that 50 percent of the candidates for the English examination (which was compulsory) passed and 50 percent failed. The pass rates of the other subjects were set in relation to the English marks, with the result that some subjects (Latin and physics, for example) had high pass rates, while others (home economics, woodwork, agriculture, and Māori, for example) had very low pass rates. The differential valuing of subjects—and students—was carried over into the internally assessed Sixth Form Certificate, because the Sixth Form Certificate grades allocated to schools were generated from the previous year group's School Certificate marks. While some of these practices were modified in the last few years of this system, some important assumptions—that these examinations measure general ability and that some subjects are harder than others—remained, and have persisted in the present system.

The NCEA is a completely different system. It is a standards-based system, which means that each student's performance in a given subject area is assessed according to whether or not their work meets a certain predetermined standard, not according to how they compare with other students in the same cohort. A wider range of assessment types is now used, although written tests and examinations are still common, especially in some subject areas, and much of the assessment is 'internal'—that is, it takes place throughout the year, and is marked by the students' teachers. Instead of passing or failing School Certificate or Sixth Form Certificate, students now accumulate 'credits' for 'standards' they have 'achieved'—that is, demonstrated that they have met the required standard.

To gain a Level 1 NCEA, students have to achieve a minimum of eight credits for standards in literacy skills, a further eight credits in numeracy, and a total of 80 Level 1 credits. A Level 2 NCEA requires a minimum of 60 credits at Level 2 or higher and 20 credits at any level, while a Level 3 NCEA requires 60 Level 3 credits and 20 at Level 2 or higher (see Table 6 on p. 75). The philosophy behind this system is that it provides evidence of what a student can do (not what they can't do). It (in theory) reduces the number of students who, under the old system, would have left school with no qualifications at all, and (in theory) allows for a wider range of learning in the upper secondary school.

In regulatory terms, the NCEA's introduction produced some major changes to the senior school curriculum. The old School Certificate, Sixth Form Certificate, and Bursary course prescriptions became obsolete in 2002, 2003, and 2004, respectively, as the NCEA was implemented. Before the new qualification could be rolled out, it was necessary to write 'Achievement Standards'; that is, the pieces of work and assessment tasks that students need to complete to achieve credits in that area of learning.[64] The processes used to develop the Achievement Standards are outlined later in this section, but Table 3 (below) summarises the nature and extent of the changes that were made to the curriculum assessment and qualification structures between 1989 and 2006.

As can be seen, the assessment and qualification system was the main focus of attention in this period. Discussion of the curriculum

---

64 Students can also credit Unit Standards—other qualification units that were developed in the early days of the NQF. Many are for technical and trades-related learning areas and are managed by Industry Training Organisations (ITOs).

Table 3 Key aspects of senior secondary curriculum development and assessment, from before 1990 to 2005

	Before 1990	1990–2000	2001–2005
National Curriculum	Subject syllabuses developed by the Department of Education (for some subjects) The 'curriculum' for some senior subjects comprised course descriptions or exam prescriptions	Introduction of the *New Zealand Curriculum Framework* (1993) Writing and implementation of curriculum statements for the seven essential learning areas, and additional subject areas (1992–2000), developed by different groups contracted and monitored by the Ministry of Education	The Curriculum Stocktake The New Zealand Curriculum/Marautanga project Preparation for a revised New Zealand national curriculum—released in draft form in 2006, and final form in November 2007
Qualifications	Year 11—School Certificate Year 12—Sixth Form Certificate Year 13—Bursary	Year 11—School Certificate Year 12—Sixth Form Certificate Year 13—Bursary NQF national certificates (assessed using Unit Standards)	Year 11—NCEA Level 1 (2002) Year 12—NCEA Level 2 (2003) Year 13—NCEA Level 3 (2004) NQF national certificates (other than NCEA)
Assessment	Department of Education and University Entrance Board develop examination prescriptions for School Certificate, Sixth Form Certificate, and Bursary	NZQA develops examination prescriptions for School Certificate, University Entrance, and later Sixth Form Certificate and Bursary Unit Standards developed and registered with NZQA (including some specifically for school subjects)	NCEA Achievement Standards developed by the Ministry of Education and registered with NZQA Standards for Entrance to University are developed for the new NCEA qualification
Legislation	1989 Education Amendment Act (Section 60A) defines the National Education Guidelines as having three components: National Educational Goals (NEGs); National Curriculum Statements; and National Administration Guidelines (NAGs)	1998 Education Amendment Act: • revokes the 1975 Instruction Regulations, which regulated curriculum in Years 9–11 • allows the gazetting of new curriculum statements to specify a 'transition period' between old syllabuses and the new curriculum statement • adds a fourth component to the NEGs: Foundation curriculum policy statements. This allows for a document like NZCF to be gazetted November 1999: further revisions to the NAGs, taking effect from July 2000	November 2001: further changes to the NEGs, mainly relating to the nature and purpose of school charters, and requirements for school planning and reporting.

was largely on the back burner, with the result that it is, we think, currently a rather odd combination of ideas inherited from its prior history and generated from the new assessment and qualifications system. This pragmatic approach to the NCEA's development has maintained some unresolved tensions from the previous senior secondary curriculum, while at the same time generating some new issues. Its introduction has been controversial because it challenges many long—and deeply—held beliefs about the purposes of senior secondary education.

One area that has been the focus of criticism is the system's emphasis on students meeting—or not meeting—prespecified standards, independently of other students. Although students can achieve each Achievement Standard at three levels (achieved, merit, and excellence), these different grades were not, until recently, recognised on the official certificate that was awarded.[65] In other words, unlike the old system, it is a system that is *not* specifically designed to sort people. Some commentators have argued that it is impossible to reliably assess students' knowledge and skills in a given subject area through a system that requires that subject to be broken down into a series of prespecified learning outcomes.[66] Others question the system's ability to achieve comparability of results between schools, between subjects, between Achievement Standards, and between years.[67] Still others argue that the removal of

---

65 However, in mid-2007 changes were introduced that allow the students' certificates to be endorsed if a specified number of credits have been gained from standards achieved with merit or excellence. Hipkins (2007) argues that this change adds to the already-existing divide in the perceived value of Unit Standards relative to Achievement Standards, in that only the latter can count for NCEA awards with merit or excellence.
66 See, for example, Hall (1999). Hall distinguishes the assessment of the learning of foundational knowledge and skills—in, for example, training situations—from the learning of more open-ended and/or contestable forms of knowledge.
67 See, for example, Elley (2003, 2005); Elley, Hall, & Marsh (2004); Nash (2005).

competition between students has been 'demotivating', particularly for more 'able' students.[68]

However, none of these arguments address the *curriculum* question that is the subject of this book. We think it is time to focus on the curriculum rather than the assessment system; to look at some of the decisions that have been made, and to evaluate the degree of fit between these decisions and the needs of 21st century learners.

How should this discussion begin? What role do the national curriculum documents play in the senior curriculum? What role *should* they play? Should there be an overarching framework to link—and give direction to—the different elements of the curriculum at this level? We explore these questions in Part 3. In the next section, however, we look at the relationship between the national curriculum documents (the 'official' curriculum) and the curriculum as experienced by Years 11–13 students in schools (the 'school' curriculum).

The national curriculum documents and the Years 11–13 'school' curriculum

Until late 2007 the NZCF was the official document designed to link and give direction to the seven 'essential learning areas'. This document was constructed, not as a curriculum statement, but as a 'foundational curriculum policy statement': that is, it did not have the legal status of a mandated curriculum. Each of the seven essential learning areas had its own national curriculum statement, developed during the 1990s (see Table 4 on p. 59). Until recently, these national curriculum statements were the only documents to have formal legal status with respect to the national curriculum, via the NEGs and the Education Amendment Act 1998, and then only up to Year 10. In practice, however, a number of other documents effectively had

---

68 See, for example, Meyer et al. (2006).

Table 4 The pre-2007 New Zealand Curriculum documents

National curriculum statements

The legally mandated curriculum

Mathematics in the New Zealand Curriculum (1992)
Science in the New Zealand Curriculum (1993)
English in the New Zealand Curriculum (1994)
Social Studies in the New Zealand Curriculum (1997)
Health and PE in the New Zealand Curriculum (1999)
Technology in the New Zealand Curriculum (1999)
The Arts in the New Zealand Curriculum (2000)

Pāngarau i Roto i te Marautanga o Aotearoa (1996)
Pūtaiao i Roto i te Marautanga o Aotearoa (1996)
Te reo Māori: i Roto i te Marautanga o Aotearoa (1996)
Tikanga ā Iwi (2000)
Hauora i Roto i te Marautanga o Aotearoa (2000)
Hangarau i Roto i te Marautanga o Aotearoa (1999)
Ngā toi: i Roto i te Marautanga o Aotearoa (2000)

Curriculum statements

Chemistry in the New Zealand Curriculum (1994)
Physics in the New Zealand Curriculum (1994)
Biology in the New Zealand Curriculum (1994)
Chinese in the New Zealand Curriculum (1995)
Spanish in the New Zealand Curriculum (1995)
Samoan in the New Zealand Curriculum (1996)
Japanese in the New Zealand Curriculum (1998)
French in the New Zealand Curriculum (2002)
German in the New Zealand Curriculum (2002)
Korean in the New Zealand Curriculum (2002)
Cook Islands Māori in the New Zealand Curriculum (2004)

Other Ministry of Education curriculum documents—(guidelines etc.)

Guidelines for Environmental Education in New Zealand Schools (1999)

Other syllabus/curriculum documents—status unclear

NZCETA Accounting Curriculum Statement for New Zealand Schools
Economics Syllabus Forms 3 to 7 (1990)
Graphics Education: Guidelines for Years 9–13 (2001)
Form 5–7 History Syllabus (1989)
Syllabus for Music Education, Early Childhood to Form 7 (1987)
Geography, Forms 5–7: Syllabus for schools (1990)

some degree of official status in New Zealand's national curriculum. These included:
- seven national curriculum statements in te reo Māori for seven essential learning areas
- curriculum statements for physics, biology, chemistry, and eight languages other than English or New Zealand Māori (i.e., subjects that are not essential learning areas)
- a number of other statements or crosscurricular guideline documents published by the Ministry of Education since 1992 (e.g., the *Guidelines for Environmental Education in New Zealand Schools*)
- several other subject syllabus and curriculum documents produced before the national curriculum statements and not specifically superseded by these.

Table 4 above (p. 59) lists the different curriculum documents that made up New Zealand's official school curriculum until late 2007.

In 2006 a draft new national curriculum was released for consultation, and the final version of this new curriculum was officially launched in November 2007. This document, which replaces the NZCF, has greater legal status. It and its partner document, *Te Marautanga o Aotearoa*, are together now the official New Zealand school curriculum. These two documents provide an overview of the entire curriculum for school students, including Achievement Objectives, for all eight learning areas ('learning languages' has been added to the previous NZCF's list of seven). The curriculum statements for each learning area, along with other yet-to-be-developed supporting materials, will become second-tier resources to support and guide teachers as they develop programmes for their students.

However, as already noted, in practice the NZCF did not set the direction for learning in Years 11–13. What then should we expect of the 2007 curriculum document? Should we expect to see changes in the senior secondary curriculum as a result of its introduction? (The document makes it quite clear (in the title and at various points in the text) that schools are required to apply it right through to Year 13.)

The NEGs, NAGs, and 1993 NZCF required schools to provide a 'balanced' curriculum for all students in all of the years of their schooling. In Years 1–10 schools are required to provide a 'broad and balanced curriculum', and to ensure that 'all students undertake continuous study in all the learning areas during each of the first ten years of schooling'.[69] Senior secondary schools, on the other hand, while their students *should* experience a balanced curriculum, with the *opportunity* to continue studies in each of the different learning areas, have not been *required* to do this. The result is that the senior secondary curriculum is currently, as it was in the past, more a collection of parts than a coherent whole.

The national curriculum statements for the 1993 document's essential learning areas were designed to guide teaching and assessment in each of these areas for *all* levels of schooling. However, in practice, as already noted, a wide range of other documents inform the current Years 11–13 curriculum. Between the mid-1990s and 2004, curriculum statements were developed for senior secondary subjects that were not part of the seven essential learning areas: notably the three senior specialist science subjects (biology, chemistry, and physics)[70] and a number of languages (see Table 4). In the traditional senior secondary curriculum, these subjects played an important role, hence there was powerful support for their continuation. However, other senior subjects—some traditional and some emerging—are *not* covered by the seven essential learning areas, and do not have their own national curriculum statements (economics, media studies, accounting, history, and geography, for example).

---

69 Ministry of Education (1993), p. 8.
70 However, generalist Years 11, 12, or 13 science courses were developed by many schools using *Science in the New Zealand Curriculum*.

Should these subjects have separate national curriculum statements? Or should we be moving away from the traditional emphasis on discrete subjects areas, instead focusing on trying to develop a more holistic and unified senior secondary curriculum? Again, these questions are addressed in Part 3 of this book. Next, however, we look at how the national curriculum statements (the 'official' planned curriculum) are interpreted at the next level down, in the 'school curriculum'. Which subjects are offered in Years 11–13? What is the relationship between these subjects and the national curriculum; that is, the curriculum framework and the curriculum statements discussed in this section? What does the individual curriculum of each Year 11, 12, or 13 student look like? What subjects—and combinations of subjects—are being offered and chosen? Are there any interesting patterns in these choices?

The school curriculum

Each year the Ministry of Education collects data from all schools about student subject enrolments. The ministry groups these subjects into eight categories, which more or less reflect the structure of the New Zealand Curriculum: languages (including English); mathematics; science; health and physical education; social studies; technology; visual and performing arts; and 'other' subjects. Table 5 shows the subjects taken by senior students in New Zealand schools in 2006; that is, the full range of subjects that were potentially available to Years 11–13 students.

Table 5 Subjects taken by students in Years 11–13 in 2006[71]

	Subjects
Languages	English, English as a second language, te reo Māori, Japanese, French, German, communication skills, Spanish, English (remedial), Samoan, Chinese, Latin, te reo Rangatira, other languages, Pacific language studies, Korean, Indonesian, Cook Island Māori, Niuean, Tongan
Mathematics	Mathematics, accounting, mathematics with statistics, mathematics with calculus, mathematics (remedial)
Science	Science, biology/biological science, physics, chemistry, agriculture/horticulture, earth science/astronomy, human biology
Social studies	Geography, history, economics, classics/classical studies, media studies, other social sciences, social studies, community studies, Māori studies, language and cultural studies
Health and physical education	Physical education, health and physical education, health, home economics, sports studies, outdoor education
Technology	Computer studies, graphics, text and information management, technology, food technology, materials technology, information and communication technology, design, drawing and graphics, textiles/clothing, electronics and control, computer science/programming, structures and mechanisms, biotechnology
Visual and performing arts	Visual arts, drama, music/music studies, photography, art design, painting, the arts, art history, music practical/performance, performing arts, dance, sculpture, printmaking
Other	Religious education/studies, life skills/personal development, study skills, transition/pre-employment, commerce-related, travel, hospitality, tourism, industrial trades, special needs programme, service trade, legal/law-related studies, farming, remedial studies, forestry, fishing.

This information does not tell us how these subjects relate to the official national curriculum. Nor does it help us to develop a picture of the curriculum offered to individual students. A large number of different subjects are offered, but obviously not all are available to all

---

71 Source: Ministry of Education, (2007), pp. 66–68.

students. Are some subjects chosen more often than others? Are there common combinations of subjects? Are there any commonalities in what is offered to senior secondary students in New Zealand?

These questions are difficult to investigate in the present system. In the past there were *de facto* patterns. Students usually took courses involving combinations of maths and science subjects; arts, humanities and language subjects; or maths and business subjects; and school timetables were structured to facilitate this. In more recent years the thinking has been that students should, if at all possible, be able to take any combination of subjects. The NZCF requires Year 11 students to take at least six subjects, 'three of which will be English or Māori, mathematics, and a science subject'. In the past, all students had to take English (or te reo Māori) for School Certificate and right through until Year 13, but Years 12 and 13 students are now allowed to make 'informed personal choices from a wide range of courses'.[72] Under the NCEA system, apart from the literacy and numeracy requirements at Level 1 (see Table 6 on p. 75 below), there are no compulsory areas of study. Students can still take one-year courses in traditional school subjects, and almost all do. However, they can also take shorter courses, take courses at different levels, and take industry-based courses. Schools can decide to make English, mathematics, or other subjects compulsory for their senior students—and some do. They can also set prerequisites for entry to various senior courses (for example, they could make certain Level 1 Achievement Standards a prerequisite for entry into certain Level 2 or 3 courses).

Thus it is possible that the curriculum offered to individual students varies considerably across the country. Is this in fact what is happening? One recent research project has investigated this question. The New Zealand Council for Educational Research (NZCER) Learning Curves Project looked at the subject and assessment choices available to senior students in six New Zealand

---

72 Ministry of Education (1993), p. 9.

secondary schools as the NQF/NCEA qualifications reforms were implemented.[73] This study found that schools were providing extensive within-subject options for students in the core curriculum subjects of mathematics, English, and science. For example, all six study schools offered two different Year 11 English courses, five offered three different mathematics courses, and all offered at least two different science courses (although science was not compulsory in all the schools). Year 11 physical education/health was compulsory in some schools. The six schools all made English compulsory to Year 12 level. The range of elective subjects offered to students varied from school to school, and the widest range of subjects offered was in the technology area. The Learning Curves schools offered different options in science, English, and mathematics to—as they saw it—best meet the different learning needs, interests, abilities, and future pathways of their students. By offering within-subject choices (in certain subjects), schools send the message that these subjects are very important and all students should take them in some form.

If the patterns found in this research are representative, then students are being offered a very large number of different options. If this is the case then, if they are to make good choices, students clearly need information and support of the highest quality. Most schools attempt to do this, although the Learning Curves work shows us that their work in this area is, to a large extent, informed by traditional understanding of the senior secondary school's purposes. There are, we think, some potentially troubling patterns in the array of subjects being taken by different groups of students. It seems that schools are—explicitly or implicitly—channelling students into subject options and combinations that are, in their view, most suitable for those students.[74] However, what is suitable, and how is the student's suitability evaluated? (See the box below for more on the Learning Curves Project's findings).

---

73 Hipkins, Vaughan, Beals, Ferral, & Gardiner (2005).
74 Vaughan & Hipkins. Unpublished.

The Learning Curves Project: the consequences of students' subject choices?

The Learning Curves researchers* carried out cluster analyses of the 2003 data from the six Learning Curves schools to investigate whether there were identifiable patterns in senior secondary students' subject choice groupings. The analyses showed that there were marked patterns in the subject choices and combinations taken by different groups of Year 11 students. These subject clusters were linked to the Year 11 English or mathematics course taken by students. For example:

- students taking the most traditional academic forms of English and mathematics tended to also take other traditional academic subjects (history and geography, economics and accounting, and/or the specialist science subjects)
- students taking more 'contextually-focused'** versions of English and mathematics were likely to also be taking applied, transition, and/or vocationally oriented technology subjects and
- there was a cluster of students who were taking ESOL English, traditional mathematics, and a mixture of academic, alternative, and practical subjects.

This analysis suggests that while the NCEA system allows for a great deal of flexibility in the courses and subjects that students can take, students are in fact being streamed into particular subject combinations. When these clusters are correlated against student characteristics such as school, gender, and ethnicity, other issues arise. For example, the students who were taking traditional English, traditional mathematics, and mostly academic subjects were mainly Pākehā. Pacific Nations and Māori students predominated in the subject cluster containing ESOL and/or alternative English and mathematics, Māori, and practical/applied subjects, and a significant number of Asian students were found in a cluster containing ESOL and/or alternative English, traditional mathematics, sciences, economics, and accounting. The analysis also showed gendered patterns of subject choice (but this could be a sample effect: two of the six schools were single-sex schools).***

The Learning Curves study involved only six schools. However, more recent findings from other NZCER work (the Competent Learners @ 16 project, involving students in around 60 schools)**** show a similar pattern. This work suggests that there may be value in extending this type of cluster analysis to a much larger data set of New Zealand students' subject combinations to investigate the extent of this pattern in other schools and possible reasons for it.

* Hipkins et al. (2004).
** The Learning Curves report defines 'contextually-focused' subject options as those that have evolved from courses that would once have been categorised as vocational or applied. These courses make closer links to students' everyday life contexts or to contexts of future work or leisure. They have the following assessment-for-qualifications characteristics: assessment is mainly by Unit Standards; a reduced number of credits is offered; and assessment is exclusively or predominantly internally managed—students seldom sit end-of-year national examinations. The division of the curriculum into topics may or may not reflect traditional partitioning of knowledge, and there is an emphasis on skills and doing, rather than recalling and reproducing knowledge.
*** See Hipkins et al. (2005) for more details of this analysis.
**** Wylie & Hipkins (in press).

More recent NZCER work provides some evidence of the extent of subject innovation now that the NCEA has bedded in. Of 124 schools completing an online survey in mid-2007, 94 percent reported having at least one subject innovation in their senior secondary school courses (that is, new courses that combine knowledge from different traditional subjects to address a specific high-level theme—environmental education, for example). However, as the Learning Curves Project found, assessment innovations (traditional subjects assessed in different ways for different learning needs) were more common than subject innovations.[75]

What does all this tell us? We think it shows that we are seeing the replacement of the old system, in which performance in the traditional subjects of the general academic curriculum was used to sort people, by a system in which the sorting is done via judgements made by subject and/or careers/guidance teachers. Is this a good thing? Answering this adequately requires us to first decide what we think the upper secondary years are *for*. We need a consensus on this before we begin to evaluate the robustness of the sorting systems. The next section looks further at the NCEA's effect on the senior secondary curriculum. Interestingly, the interaction between traditional ideas about the purposes of the upper secondary years and the new assessment regime appears to be producing a system that assesses using standards while, at the same time, continuing to rank students.

The assessed curriculum

The implementation of the NCEA has, to some extent, disrupted traditional thinking about assessment. However, as the Learning Curves research shows, it has not affected the curriculum to the extent we might have expected. This section reviews the evolution of the NCEA model in the context of the New Zealand Qualifications

---

75 See Hipkins (2007).

Framework that produced it, and explores its effects on curriculum development.

In today's system, New Zealand secondary school students work towards one of several NZQA national certificates. The National Certificate of Educational Achievement, or NCEA, is one of these certificates, but there are others in specialist areas. All NZQA national certificates are recognised on the NQF. These national certificates use standards-based assessment. Students work towards certain prespecified learning outcomes—clear statements of what students should know and do (in that learning area, at that level). As students achieve specific outcomes, they receive credits, and when a student has sufficient credits at specified levels and in specified subjects, the qualification is awarded. As we have seen, two types of standards are used in the NQF: Unit Standards (developed from the early 1990s onwards) and Achievement Standards (developed from the late 1990s onwards). Why are there two different standards? What is the difference between them? What effect has their development had on the senior secondary curriculum? We look at each of these questions below.

Unit Standards

Thousands of Unit Standards, in areas from automotive electrical mechanics and community development, to geography and biology, have been developed. Generally speaking, two different kinds of Unit Standards are used in schools:
1. Unit Standards developed by ITOs
2. approved curriculum-related Unit Standards.

The development of ITO-produced Unit Standards and qualifications for use in trade and technical qualifications was the initial focus of the 1990s qualifications policy reforms. ITOs and other education and training providers developed Unit Standards that were appropriate to their fields. In the mid-1990s educationists began to develop standards-based forms of assessment for senior school subjects. By 1993/94 the Unit Standards development work was widened to include school subjects and other learning areas that did not fit clearly into one field of industry. These were called the curriculum-related Unit Standards. NZQA began establishing advisory groups, some of which were later amalgamated into national standards bodies (NSBs), to develop standards and qualifications in these areas.[76]

At the time it was anticipated that some form of standards-based system would eventually replace School Certificate, Sixth Form Certificate, and University Bursary.[77] This was not a new idea: reforms to senior secondary assessment and qualification practices had been called for—and deferred—for decades.[78] For example, in the 1980s a great deal of effort (and investment in teacher professional development) went into developing what was then called Achievement Based Assessment systems for senior secondary biology, physical education, and geography. These systems were trialled, but not pursued. Unit Standards were, however, eventually developed for many of the conventional secondary subjects. One result of this was that for some years the assessment of senior secondary students' learning could involve *either* Unit Standards-based assessment, *or* the exam-based awards, or both. Teachers and schools who chose to assess students with Unit Standards (most often in Sixth Form Certificate subjects) saw this as an opportunity to assess aspects of students' learning that weren't formally acknowledged in the exam-based system that predominated at the time. This hybrid system eventually came to an end with the introduction of the NCEA.

---

76 New Zealand Government (1999).
77 NZQA (2000).
78 See, for example, Strachan (2001).

The introduction of the NQF, and the development and uptake of Unit Standards in secondary schools, was significant for the senior secondary curriculum for several reasons. First, because industry groups and vocational and technical education providers were involved in developing qualifications and standards, these groups now had a legitimate role to play in shaping the school curriculum. Second, Unit Standards and the NQF provided a more visible way to recognise and accredit educational achievement in areas outside the traditional academic subject areas; in particular, in vocationally oriented learning areas such as automotive engineering, catering, or tourism. These areas were now recognised as learning that counted towards students' education and qualification pathways. This created some tensions around who is—and should be—qualified to teach or to assess standards that have been developed by industry or other training providers. For example, the journalism ITO that developed Unit Standards for print journalism apparently insisted that these be taught by registered journalists, not English teachers.[79] Conversely, teachers often find industry-developed Unit Standards are not entirely suitable for the needs of their students, and schools often have difficulty finding resources to support the teaching of some Unit Standards and/or finding moderators to assist in assessing them.[80]

Many teachers saw Unit Standards as valuable for formative assessment or assessment-for-learning for their students. However, the continued coexistence of the Unit Standards/NQF alongside the old exam-based qualifications raised some difficult issues. The government's *White Paper* on the NQF noted concerns among students, teachers, and parents that:

> ... some students are being assessed against Unit Standards for NQF qualifications, as well as being prepared for examination-based awards

---

79 Horrocks & Hoben (2005), p. 5.
80 Boyd, McDowall, & Cooper (2002).

such as School Certificate and Bursary in the same subjects. This has proved confusing and onerous for teachers, and some have felt that the Unit Standards have not adequately recognised or rewarded excellence.[81]

Concern was expressed that the combination of exam-based assessment and Unit Standards was creating an unequal 'two-tier' system.[82] The proposed solution to this was to develop a new senior secondary qualification, the NCEA, and new kinds of standards, known as Achievement Standards.

Achievement Standards

In November 1998, as part of the *Achievement 2001* initiative, the Minister of Education announced that the National Certificate of Educational Achievement would replace all existing Years 11–13 qualifications, and, following from this, that a new kind of standard was needed for assessing the conventional subjects—that is, the nationally recognised School Certificate, Sixth Form Certificate, and University Bursary subjects.

How were the Achievement Standards developed?

The development of Achievement Standards in the late 1990s was directed and overseen by the Ministry of Education's Qualifications Development Group. Various decisions made at this time—about how the Achievement Standards would be developed and the areas of learning they were needed for—were pivotal in shaping the senior curriculum from that point onwards. The official message given to schools and the public was that the changeover to NCEA was *not* going to substantially change the curriculum, beyond broadening the range of options and possibilities for students. Given the scale of change involved with the NCEA's implementation (along with other major

---

81 New Zealand Government (1999).
82 NZQA (2000).

curriculum changes in other areas of the school), it is hardly surprising that teachers, students, and the public wanted to be reassured that there would be continuity of teaching and learning in the core subjects when the new assessment regime was implemented. Thus the process for developing Achievement Standards emphasised the *conservation* of existing practices and ideas about the senior curriculum.

It was decided that Achievement Standards would be developed for all of the old School Certificate, Sixth Form Certificate, and University Bursary subjects,[83] as well as a few subjects that were not School Certificate or Bursary subjects, but had curriculum statements (e.g., social studies), and at least one subject (media studies) that had neither a curriculum statement nor a prior existence as a Bursary subject.[84]

The Qualifications Development Group convened specialist panels of expert educators in each learning area of the curriculum.[85] Each expert panel, comprising up to 24 members, was to meet three times. At the first meeting, the panels were to decide which areas the Achievement Standards should cover, and to draft a matrix for Achievement Standards development for all four NCEA levels in its learning area.[86] NCEA policy was that at least half the Achievement Standards for each subject would be externally assessable through examinations or other forms of external assessment. In developing the Achievement Standards, the expert panels were supposed to refer to 'curriculum documents, exam prescriptions, Unit Standards, and the best of current classroom practice'.[87] These working groups

---

83 Ministry of Education (1999b).
84 Media studies was a Sixth Form Certificate subject and there had been a history of lobbying for it to become a Bursary subject. It was probably on this basis that it was included in the list of subjects to have Achievement Standards developed. See Horrocks and Hoben (2005).
85 Panel positions were publicly advertised through subject associations and in the *Education Gazette*, and shortlists of candidates were selected from more than 800 expressions of interest. See Ministry of Education (1999b).
86 NCEA Levels 1, 2, 3, and Scholarship (Level 4).
87 Ministry of Education (1999a), p. 1.

drafted and refined Achievement Standards, which were then sent to all schools for critique. This feedback was analysed, synthesised, and reported back to the working parties, and adjustments were recommended. The finalised Achievement Standards were then sent to NZQA for quality assurance and final registration on the NQF.[88]

What does an Achievement Standard look like?

Achievement Standards are specified at four levels (Levels 1, 2, and 3 on the NQF, plus University Scholarship level). There is a total of 24 credits[89] available for any subject at Levels 1, 2, and 3. NCEA policy is that there should be between five and eight Achievement Standards for each subject. Each Achievement Standard is assigned a credit value as a proportion of the total 24 available for that subject at that level. Thus most are worth two, three, or four credits. Achievement Standards are currently used only for NCEA subjects (see Appendix A for a list of the 30 subjects with Achievement Standards).

Similarities and differences between Unit Standards and Achievement Standards

Achievement Standards are similar to Unit Standards in that they set out criteria for assessing student performance. In general, both types of standards do not prescribe content or the full texture of a curriculum, nor do they prescribe exactly how assessments are to be carried out.[90] However, the two standards differ in some important ways:

- Unit Standards are all internally assessed. In contrast, Achievement Standards can be assessed by examination (or other external

---

88 Tim McMahon and Ann Greenaway (Ministry of Education), personal communications.
89 The rule of 24 credits per subject was determined by comparison with the credit value of Unit Standards. A full Sixth Form programme was considered to comprise 120 credits. Divided by 5 (the usual number of subjects taken in Sixth Form) this yields a value of 24 possible credits per subject.
90 NZQA (2001).

assessment) or internally. (This is specified for each standard, although examiners and schools can decide on appropriate assessment tasks and activities within this structure.)
- Unit Standards can only be 'achieved' or 'not achieved'. In contrast, Achievement Standards can be achieved at three levels: 'achieved', 'achieved with merit', or 'achieved with excellence'. Students are not given additional credits for achieving a standard with merit or excellence, but their grade averages for a subject are raised.
- Achievement Standards tend to be broader and leaner than Unit Standards, in that in general they have fewer specific performance criteria.

How students gain the NCEA

In 1999 a group called the Secondary Sector Forum, made up of school principals, teachers, and tertiary and industry sector representatives, was established to provide advice on issues relating to the introduction of the NCEA. This group recommended that all achievement, in whatever field, should count towards a certificate, which would be awarded once sufficient credit had been obtained, regardless of source.[91] The forum also recommended that students be required to achieve some specified level of literacy and numeracy before they were awarded a Level 1 NCEA.[92] Table 6 below sets out the requirements for gaining an NCEA at Levels 1, 2, and 3.

---

91 Ministry of Education (1999a).
92 *Ibid.*

Table 6 Requirements for gaining NCEA (as at December 2005)

NCEA Level 1	NCEA Level 2	NCEA Level 3
• 80 credits at Level 1 or higher (achieved through Unit Standards or Achievement Standards) • 8 credits from approved standards for literacy skills* • 8 credits from approved standards for numeracy skills**	• 60 credits at Level 2 or higher • 20 credits at any level***	• 60 credits at Level 3 or higher • 20 credits at Level 2 or higher****

* These are specified on the NZQA website.
** These are specified on the NZQA website.
*** These 20 credits may include credits which counted towards the Level 1 Certificate.
**** These 20 credits may include credits which counted towards the Level 2 Certificate.

Entrance requirements for university

The changes to New Zealand's senior secondary curriculum and assessment have been paralleled by changes to the entrance requirements for university. Before 1986 there were two Year 12 qualifications: University Entrance and Sixth Form Certificate.[93] Students who wanted to go to university could gain University Entrance[94] in Year 12, or they could stay at school and sit Bursary examinations in Year 13. Most stayed on to Year 13.

In 1986 the University Entrance qualification was dropped, and the University Bursary examination became the gatekeeper of university entrance. By the mid-1990s, when it was becoming clear that the old examination system would eventually be replaced by a standards-

---

93 Sixth Form Certificate was originally developed to allow schools to provide a more comprehensive range of courses than was available from University Entrance subjects. In general, there was no direct connection between University Entrance and Sixth Form Certificate. See NZQA (2004).
94 Students could gain University Entrance either by sitting University Entrance examinations, or, if their school was approved as an accrediting school, by reaching a satisfactory standard through a programme of internal assessment.

based system, a working party was set up to develop a standards-based model for university entrance. This process was then put on hold, pending various government decisions on the timing and exact nature of the phasing out of University Bursary.[95] The working party was reconvened in the late 1990s when the decision was taken to replace the University Bursary examination with Level 3 NCEA, complete with Unit Standards and the new Achievement Standards. This working party, made up of representatives from NZQA,[96] the New Zealand Vice Chancellors' Committee, the Ministry of Education, and school principals, was asked to develop a model for university entrance under the NCEA. The working party considered several different models,[97] noted calls for literacy and numeracy standards to be built into the university entrance requirements, and sought feedback on the literacy and numeracy skills needed for success at university. It went on to argue that the traditional 'canon of subjects' was an important part of the preparation for degree-level study.[98] This group of subjects became known as the 'Vice Chancellors' list' of 'approved subjects' (see Appendix B). The university entrance working party eventually decided on a standard for university entrance, which was to operate for two years.[99] This interim standard is shown below.

---

95 NZQA (2000). However, growth in Unit Standard uptake in secondary schools led in 1998 to the establishment of an interim standard for university entrance. Successful candidates could gain university entrance by gaining either: 13 credits at Level 3 on the NQF in three approved subjects, as well as Higher School Certificate; or three C passes in Bursary subject exams, as well as Higher School Certificate; or a combination of credits in approved subjects and C passes in Bursary exams; or an A or B Bursary.
96 Section 257 of the Education Act 1989 requires the NZQA to set a common standard for entrance to university. In doing so, it must consult with the universities and the New Zealand Vice Chancellors' Committee.
97 NZQA (2000).
98 Ministry of Education (2000a).
99 In 2004 NZQA announced a process and time frame for reviewing the university entrance standard. See NZQA (2004).

The requirements to qualify for university entrance (as at December 2005)

> The requirements are:
> 1. a minimum of 42 credits at Level 3 or higher on the NQF, including a minimum of 14 credits at Level 3 or higher in each of two subjects from the 'approved subjects' list, with a further 14 credits at Level 3 or higher taken from one or two additional domains on the NQF or approved subjects
> 2. a minimum of 14 numeracy credits at Level 1 or higher in mathematics or pangarau on the NQF
> 3. a minimum of eight literacy credits at Level 2 or higher in English or te reo Māori; four credits must be in reading and four credits must be in writing.

Interestingly, under this standard, the requirements for university entrance are *separate* from the requirements for the NCEA: that is, students can gain NCEA without necessarily being eligible for university entrance, and vice versa. Thus there are potential difficulties for students here: each student's proposed course must be thoroughly checked by someone with extensive knowledge of the regulations if students are to avoid 'wasting a year' (by gaining an NCEA that does not allow them entry to university).

How have these changes affected the curriculum offered to senior secondary school students? The short answer is: not as much as might have been expected. The traditional model outlined earlier in this book, in which the senior school curriculum was *entirely* focused on university preparation, has been replaced by one that offers a wider range of subjects, prepares students for a wider range of postschool pathways, and is, in theory, assessed very differently. However, in practice, the university system still strongly influences the overall shape and focus of the curriculum, and we still have the old two-tier system of high-value and low-value subjects.

Plus ça change, plus c'est la même chose …

In this section we have surveyed the significant and complex changes made in recent years to the structures that frame senior secondary school education. What strikes us, in taking this bird's-eye view, is that while there is no doubt that the structural changes have been massive, because the deeper ideas that underlie—and drive—what we do in the senior secondary school haven't changed very much, what happens to students hasn't changed very much either.

Is this good or bad? Again the answer depends on what we want our secondary schools to do. What kind of people—with what kinds of knowledge and skills—do we want them to produce, and why? In the last part of this book we explore some of these issues.

PART THREE

WHERE TO FROM HERE?
SOME OPTIONS FOR THE FUTURE

Over the last 20 years or so, New Zealand's senior secondary education system has undergone substantial change. The relatively straightforward traditional framework (represented in Figure 1 on p. 20) has been added to and modified in response to a range of new ideas and pressures. Today's senior secondary curriculum (represented in Figure 2 on p. 42) is a much more complex system. Students are offered a wide range of different study options and pathways, both through the system and at the end of it. While these changes have been welcomed and accepted by many in the school sector and wider educational community, they have been strongly contested by others. A number of compromises have been necessary, with the result that the current system is framed around an odd mixture of competing—and sometimes conflicting—ideas and philosophies. In this section we look at some of the implications of this.

We begin by making four general observations about recent developments in New Zealand's senior secondary curriculum, as a way of raising some questions for discussion by policy makers, secondary school leaders, teachers, and anyone else with an involvement or stake in senior secondary education. We then look at four key elements of the old system that, we think, actively prevent change and show how these elements could be reframed to contribute to a 21st century education system.

The senior secondary curriculum since 1990—four key themes

Theme one: deciding by default

The first of our four general observations is that, since the 1990s, many of the decisions about the curriculum at senior secondary level have been made as a result of *other* decisions; that is, they have been made not as *curriculum* decisions, but following developments in other areas, particularly assessment and qualifications. While decisions about what to assess and how to assess are, in effect, curriculum decisions, we think the cart has been put before the horse. This is nothing new: for most of the 20th century educationists complained that the examination system had too much influence on what was taught. What *is* new is the advent of the Knowledge Age and other major changes in the world beyond education. These changes throw this old problem into sharp relief. Our focus on redeveloping the assessment and qualifications system *before* paying attention to the curriculum has left traditional assumptions about what students should learn in the final years of their secondary education unquestioned. We think we should work out *what* students need to learn if they are to be adequately prepared for life and work in the 21st century (and why these things are important) *before* we try to work out how best to assess whether or not they have learnt them.

For example, one key decision in the 1990s was to develop a broad array of Unit Standards for a whole range of learning areas not available in the traditional curriculum. Underpinning this was the idea that there should be a wide range of different curriculum options available to senior secondary learners, and—implicitly—the idea that there is some sort of problem with the traditional curriculum (for example, that it is too narrow, not relevant, or too hard for some students). Another key decision, made slightly later, was to develop Achievement Standards for the existing School Certificate/ University Bursary subjects. As noted earlier, this decision was taken to some extent as a way of reducing the overall burden of change. However, at the same time, it also represents a commitment to treating the traditional academic subjects as the *appropriate* core of any reasonable senior secondary school programme.

How should we interpret this decision in relation to the earlier one? Are the traditional academic subjects still to be valued or not? Are they only suitable for some people? What was the *real* purpose of the changes? At one level, the decision to expand the range of study options was probably connected to the 1993 decision to raise the school-leaving age to 16 years.[100] Our search of publicly available documents has not provided an answer to the question of why this was thought to be a good idea (apart from the fact that it brought us into line with the UK).[101] It could be that these decisions were an attempt to have a bet both ways: to better meet the needs of a wider range of students while at the same time also preserving the status quo of the traditional academic curriculum.

This hedging of bets approach avoids—rather than solves—some key issues. For example, does the notion of wider curriculum choice mean that we are dispensing with the idea of a common core for *all* senior secondary learners; the idea that some forms of knowledge and some skills are needed by *everyone*? Currently the only compulsory areas of learning at the senior level are basic literacy and numeracy. To be awarded a Level 1 NCEA all students must achieve a specified number of credits from a range of standards in English and mathematics.[102] Is this enough? Does the development of the different types of standards in different learning areas preclude the possibility of developing a coherent framework that might link and give direction to the senior curriculum as a whole? Should this be a goal? And, importantly, we think, was the implicit replication of the traditional division between academic and applied forms of knowledge a conscious decision, or did it just happen as an unintended by-product of other decisions?

The management and resourcing issues involved in implementing these decisions have received some attention, but we think it is time

---

100 The school-leaving age was raised to 16 by the 1991 Education Amendment Act. This took effect on 1 January 1993. See Ministry of Education (1992).
101 All we found was a great deal of information on the transition options that would need to be in place to support this move.
102 However, the exact standards are not specified, so there is not really any central core of key knowledge.

to evaluate the long-term implications of these decisions for the curriculum, for students, and for the country as a whole. There are some signs[103] that this work is starting to happen.

Theme two: the devolution of senior secondary curriculum decisions

Our second general observation is that the processes for creating and updating senior secondary subjects have been decentralised. Traditionally (before the introduction of the NCEA), most senior secondary subjects were constructed in a top-down way from the university disciplines. Each subject was a distinct entity, controlled by a separate group of experts and a separate process. New subjects—media studies, journalism, or Bursary physical education, for example—were sometimes created as a result of pressure from groups of teachers (sometimes with the support of university academics),[104] and could become nationally recognised School Certificate, Sixth Form Certificate, or University Bursary subjects if they gained central approval (from the Department of Education, NZQA, or the University Entrance Board). There were also local courses, especially for Sixth Form Certificate, that were not centrally designed, although schools had to submit course statements and assessment procedures for NZQA approval.

Existing subjects could be updated in two ways. Periodic revisions of the centrally controlled School Certificate and University Bursary subject prescriptions helped subjects keep up with contemporary developments in the discipline (e.g., new knowledge, or new ways of thinking about the discipline). Alternatively, local versions of conventional subjects could be developed to meet the needs of particular groups of students. These could sit outside the Ministry of Education/NZQA-managed qualifications registered on the NQF.

---

103 For example, in recent work on the New Zealand Curriculum/Marautanga Project, and on the Secondary Futures project.

104 See Horrocks and Hoben (2005) for an account of the emergence of media studies in secondary schools in the early 1980s.

One example of this is the Certificate in Science, an alternative Year 11 course which was developed for the New Zealand Association of Science Educators (NZASE) from a UK model by a panel of New Zealand science teachers.[105]

Thus, before the advent of the NCEA, senior secondary courses were largely centrally controlled, and the individual subjects were discrete entities, organised to be approximately equal in size (in terms of the number of hours required to complete the course). However, since the NCEA system was implemented, things have changed. There are now no whole-course examination prescriptions to act as *de facto* national curricula for senior secondary subjects, and as a result the traditional directly centralised regulation of the secondary school subjects has been weakened, if not abolished.[106] Schools can modify and update the subjects they offer to meet the needs of their particular group of students, or they can create entirely new subjects. Some schools are doing this, and are assessing student learning via mixtures of Unit Standards and Achievement Standards from a range of different learning areas. So far these innovations have mostly been adaptations of conventional subjects like mathematics and English.[107] While this is similar in principle to the old provision for developing local subjects for Sixth Form Certificate, schools do not now have to submit course prescriptions or assessment plans for NZQA approval. In addition, courses can differ in terms of their credit value, and therefore their size and/or workload.

Thus in theory schools can now develop their own curriculum at the senior secondary school level, without central approval.

---

105 This course originally sat outside the national system, but no longer does: NCEA Unit Standards have now been created to assess this course for NQF credits.
106 However, entrance requirements for university courses still act to maintain traditional subject categories.
107 The Learning Curves research (Hipkins et al., 2002, 2004, 2005) found that this occurred right from the very first year of the NCEA's implementation.

This devolution of control is consistent with the new *New Zealand Curriculum*'s focus on school-based curriculum development.[108] However, there are some unique features of the senior secondary school that make this theoretical flexibility to meet local needs very difficult to take up. One major constraint, at least on the surface, is the assessment system's effect on the curriculum. However, we would argue, at a deeper level, the real constraint is the persistence of old—and unexamined—ideas about the purposes of schooling at the senior secondary school level. The Learning Curves research finding that, while flexible course design is occurring in some schools in applied and/or emerging subject areas, it is much less common in the traditional academic subject areas (with the exception of the special-needs mathematics and English courses outlined above) is, we think, a very interesting indicator of some deeper assumptions. This leads us to our third theme.

Theme three: conflicting purposes of assessment at senior secondary level

Our third observation, which is related to the discussion above, is that the overhauling of the senior secondary school assessment system in a context in which old ideas about the purpose of schooling at this level persist, has produced some perverse incentives.

As outlined earlier, the new system's competency-oriented philosophy has been resisted by some[109] and even subverted,[110] questions are being raised about its ability to compare student performance across and within subjects and years,[111] and we are

---

108 Ministry of Education (2007).
109 For example, via the adoption of alternative assessment systems such as the Cambridge examination system or the International Baccalaureate examination.
110 For example, the pressure to introduce the practice of endorsing students' NCEA with merit or excellence where sufficient credits are gained at the appropriate level.
111 See, for example, Elley (2003, 2005); Elley el al. (2004); Hall (1999); Nash (2005).

seeing the emergence of a two-tier system. At the same time, we are seeing research findings that suggest that the system is demotivating for students,[112] and that it encourages students, teachers, and schools to adopt a 'fruit salad' approach to curriculum: that is, to assemble Achievement and Unit Standards to produce courses of study designed to maximise 'success' (credit accumulation), as opposed to learning via a broad and balanced curriculum.[113]

The emergence of these critiques tells us that we do not, as yet, have anything approaching a consensus on what senior secondary schooling is *for*. The old idea of secondary school as the place where students bound for university (or other tertiary study) are sorted from those heading directly into paid employment is evident in these critiques, as is the old emphasis on the traditional disciplines as both a context for training the mind (the broad and balanced curriculum) *and* as the means of sorting people. This mixture of ideas is, we think, a serious problem. This problem could be addressed in a number of ways—for example, by abolishing the approved subjects list,[114] or by requiring schools to fully implement *The New Zealand Curriculum* at Years 11–13 (as signalled in the new curriculum document)[115]—but the real problem is, we think, the lack of a coherent vision, a *new* shared understanding of the *purposes* of senior secondary schooling in the 21st century.

---

112 See, for example, Meyer et al. (2006).
113 Allison (2005).
114 See Appendix B.
115 The 2007 *New Zealand Curriculum* makes it clear that it is the official curriculum document at senior secondary level, as well as all the other levels of schooling. In the Requirements for Boards of Trustees (on p. 44), it advises that 'teaching programmes for students in Years 11–13 should be based, in the first instance, on the appropriate national curriculum statements'. However, it does not specify how (if at all) the broad Achievement Objectives for each learning area should relate to NCEA Achievement Standards and Unit Standards.

Theme four: the seamless curriculum framework?

The fourth general observation is that the relationship between the senior secondary subjects and *The New Zealand Curriculum* remains unclear. Table 5 above (p. 63) lists more than 80 subjects taken by students in Years 11–13 in New Zealand schools.[116] The subjects are grouped into categories associated with the seven essential learning areas (of the pre-2007 curriculum), plus a category of 'other' subjects. However, *do* all these subjects actually have a relationship to one of the essential learning areas? If so, what is the nature of this relationship? Why were curriculum statements *over and above* the Essential Learning Area statements produced for some senior subjects in the 1990s (e.g., biology, chemistry, physics, and the languages), but not for others (e.g., economics, media studies, or geography)?

Without having been part of the discussions that produced this state of affairs, it is hard to answer these questions. It could be that the seven[117] essential learning areas are seen as being the basis of a broad and balanced curriculum for most of the years of schooling, while providing a platform for the transition to the senior secondary years, which have a new and different set of purposes. However, what seems more likely is that, because senior secondary schooling has a set of long-established traditions and practices that relate directly to the old assessment/qualifications structures, and teachers and other stakeholders have strong investments in maintaining these, there was strong lobbying for the status quo. This, coupled with the fact that it was not actually feasible to review and revise the entire senior secondary curriculum within the time and resources available

---

116 Note that this data only tells us the generic names of the subject types taught by schools. However, in terms of content or pedagogy, there is no way of knowing how similar—or different—subjects with the same name look in different schools.
117 Note that in the 2007 curriculum there are now eight 'learning areas'.

for the reshaping of the compulsory school curriculum, could be why we have not yet dealt with the question of what senior secondary schooling should look like in the 21st century.

In the meantime, the current system has some interesting anomalies. *Should* all senior subjects have a curriculum statement? If so, *why*? Should the existing senior curriculum statements be updated to reflect the revised Achievement Objectives of the 2007 curriculum document? What underpins teaching in subjects that *don't* have a curriculum statement? These issues are discussed below.

What influences how the different subjects are taught?

Curriculum statements are not the only influence on how a subject is taught (and what is taught within it). Some other sources of influence are:

- unofficial curriculum statements or guidelines produced by subject associations (e.g., the NZCETA Accounting Curriculum Statement for New Zealand schools)
- old exam prescriptions and/or old senior subject syllabuses (pre-NZCF)
- teachers' subject knowledge and interests (e.g., as individuals, departmental groups, or subject associations)
- existing practice (e.g., school traditions, existing departmental schemes)
- guidance from tertiary education institutions and other education and training providers (e.g., the alignment of secondary subjects with tertiary courses or work-based training programmes)
- guidance, support, resources, and/or theoretical frameworks from communities of interest in particular knowledge areas outside the education sector (e.g., the biotechnology community or the environmental education community)
- other local sources of knowledge, support, and resourcing (e.g., local experts, or access to a local natural or built resource, which

can be utilised in the development of secondary curriculum subjects)
- the assessment and qualification tools available (e.g., the nature of Unit Standards or Achievement Standards that are available in a particular subject area/domain).

How—if at all—should teachers be guided when drawing from this pool of different sources? Should they try to achieve a balance between what are often conflicting ideas? Is one source better or more appropriate in educational contexts than another? Should the subject be offered in a similar form to all students taking it at that level across the country, or should teachers tailor their selection of topics and their teaching of them to the needs of their particular group of students? Is it the individual teacher's job to make these decisions? According to Judie Allison, PPTA Advisory Officer, reporting on research exploring teachers' perceptions of these issues, The New Zealand Curriculum/Marautanga project[118] has not taken enough account of the needs of senior subjects, especially those that don't have a clear link to a specific essential learning area. She says that teachers believe that there is 'no real curriculum direction any more' and that:

> ... for many of the senior subjects, there is no national statement available to teachers telling them what 'subject experts' deem to be a balanced and coherent curriculum around which they should organise their teaching and assessment (or choose to deviate from, given good reasons).[119]

This view that teachers are adrift in the absence of subject-specific curriculum documents appears to be more common among teachers of the conventional subject areas which, in the old system (depicted in

---

[118] The work that underpinned the development of the 2007 *New Zealand Curriculum*.
[119] Allison (2005), p. 1.

Figure 1 on p. 20 above), were developed from discussions between university subject experts, curriculum specialists, and teachers. It has led to pressure from teachers and their subject associations to develop national curriculum statements for subjects that don't currently have their own document, that aren't sufficiently covered within one of the Essential Learning Areas curriculum statements, or that are perceived to belong across multiple essential learning areas. Some examples are economics, media studies, classical studies, or subjects with more of a basis in industry training standards, such as travel and tourism.

Should developing (or revising) national curriculum statements for all subjects be a priority? On the one hand, there are issues of fairness, transparency, and comparability (between schools and students in the same subject, and between different subjects) when national curriculum statements do not exist for all subjects. On the other hand, the national curriculum statement concept is likely to bring with it the baggage of the old examination prescriptions: in particular, their prescriptiveness and, following from this, a closing down of innovation.

So what should we do? One possibility is to develop curriculum guidelines that do *not* recuperate the old examination prescriptions, but are instead explicitly *future* focused.

Should all senior subjects have a curriculum statement? If so, why?

What does—or could—a curriculum statement do for a subject? It can:

- give a subject status (e.g., the existence of a curriculum statement in a subject like biology suggests that, as a country, we think biology is an important subject for students to learn at secondary school)

- underpin the development of assessment tools such as Achievement Standards[120]
- provide some kind of consensus about what the subject is about and what is most important to know/do/learn/teach[121]
- express a clear and coherent philosophical approach and frame (or reframe) how teachers think about their subject.[122]

This last purpose is important for the present discussion. Traditionally, the teacher's role has been to interpret or translate the curriculum (in the secondary school context, as a series of topics or 'bits of knowledge') for the needs of their students. This model of curriculum implementation is under pressure in a time of major change. The focus, in the world outside education, on developing new knowledge and learning should lead us to re-examine some of our assumptions about knowledge and learning, and our ideas about what constitutes a successful school leaver.

The new *New Zealand Curriculum*'s foregrounding of key competencies signals a shift in thinking for the earlier years of schooling. This shift, if carried through to the senior years, could be the basis of a more future-focused senior curriculum. The current emphasis on mastering bits of knowledge as an end in itself could be replaced by an emphasis on doing things *with* bits of knowledge (or knowledge systems), on building students' skills, not in terms of reproducing old knowledge but generating *new* knowledge. The

---

120 In the development of NCEA Achievement Standards, the existing curriculum documents in each area were cited as one important source of guidance for the standards' developers.

121 This in turn raises questions about whose views are, or should be, represented in the development of curriculum statements, and whose views are typically excluded. See, for example, Bolstad (2004), McKinley & Waiti (1995), Reid (1987).

122 For an example of this in a New Zealand secondary school subject, see the discussion of changes to teaching practice in home economics in the recent *Shifting Balances* 2 research report (Hipkins, Conner, & Neill, 2006).

competencies that, in the past, were assumed to develop through exposure to the traditional disciplines—analysing, synthesising, and critical thinking, for example—could be foregrounded and *explicitly* developed, using, but also extending beyond, the old subjects. Developing national curriculum statements for each of the subjects in the senior secondary curriculum would, we think, be a useful first step in beginning to develop our ideas about what a 21st century senior school curriculum might look like. However, *before*—or possibly alongside—this work, we also need to work out a new consensus on the issue of what we want the senior secondary school curriculum to *do*. We need to find ways to think outside the square of the old ideas if we are to reconfigure our schools for 21st century needs. In the next section we suggest some ways we might begin to do this.

Developing a 21st century senior school curriculum: first steps

As outlined in Part 1 of this book, the Knowledge Society literature tells us that *all* young people need the kinds of knowledge and skills that were traditionally seen as the domain of higher education. If we accept this as a goal, then a major mind shift is required. We need new ideas about what schools are *for* (to screen, sort, and discipline students for life and work in a society organised to meet Industrial Age needs, or to help them become robust, rich, flexible, all-round learners in a fast-changing knowledge-based society), and new ideas about how schools should be organised.[123] We need to rethink current ideas about the role of the traditional disciplines in the school curriculum, and to rethink the motivational stories we give to students.

Knowledge, in the Knowledge Society, has a new meaning. Knowledge is innovation. Its role is to generate new knowledge,

---

123 See also Warner (2006).

to *do* things. If we accept this, we need to refocus the school curriculum. Instead of seeing knowledge as an end in itself, as an object for students to master and reproduce, we need to develop students' ability to work with—or do things with—knowledge. At one level this is a major shift. In practice what is needed is more of a shift in emphasis. Instead of expecting that students will pick up general intellectual skills—such as the ability to analyse, synthesise, generalise, and think creatively—through exposure to the traditional disciplines, and to transfer those skills to new contexts, a Knowledge Age curriculum needs to *explicitly* develop these skills, and some *new* ones.

The Knowledge Society literature also tells us that, while left-brain thinking, the kind of methodical, logical, sequential, analytical thinking emphasised in traditional education systems, is still important and necessary, it is no longer enough. People need to be big-picture thinkers, to be pattern recognisers and meaning makers. They need right-brain thinking skills—the ability to think metaphorically, simultaneously, aesthetically, and contextually—and, importantly, they need to be able to empathise and connect with others, to have well-developed people and relationship-building skills.[124] A curriculum designed to build these abilities would have a different emphasis from current approaches. The traditional disciplines would still be important, but *not* as ends in themselves. Instead, their role would be to provide the resources and/or contexts for developing these abilities.

We would also need to think about learning in new ways. Learning how to learn is not a new goal of education. However, in recent years we have seen an increase in discussion of this idea in a variety of different guises, including developing learning (or lifelong learning) skills, building learning capacity, developing positive learning

---

124 See Gardner (2006); Pink (2006).

dispositions, and so on. Despite all this, as yet we have not made much practical progress with *really* developing this idea, largely because we are still focused on getting students to learn specific bits of knowledge and improving their achievement on tests that measure the ability to remember and retain these bits of knowledge. Changing this requires a new orientation. First, it requires a shift away from seeing learning as 'getting' bits of knowledge; and second, it requires us to think about what building learning capacity *really* means, and how we might seriously go about doing it.[125]

While at first glance all this might look a little daunting, we don't think it necessarily is. Armed with a good understanding of where we have come from (and why we came that way), and a well-thought-out framework for organising our progress, the idea of refocusing our school curriculum for the 21st century doesn't look so difficult. We need to reconfigure the old approach for the new context. We don't need to develop—and then disseminate—entirely new practices, but to 're-grow' the old ones for the new conditions.[126]

Which old practices—or assumptions—need re-growing for the 21st century? We think there are four main areas for change:
- current ideas about the relationship between the curriculum and the disciplines
- ideas about learning
- the motivational 'stories' we tell students
- the metaphors we use to think about senior secondary education.

In the next section we look at how we might reframe these areas to fit with 21st century needs.

---

125 Claxton (2007).
126 The 're-growing' concept is taken from comments made by US education academics David Perkins and Shirley Brice Heath, quoted in Claxton (2007), p. 129.

Rethinking the discipline–curriculum relationship for 21st century secondary schools

If we accept the idea that the main purpose of schooling in the 21st century is to help young people develop the capacity to think and learn independently, and the ability to work with knowledge in an environment of constant change, then we need to rethink the conventionally tight relationship between the subjects of the senior school curriculum and the traditional disciplines. The traditional content of the school curriculum comes from disciplinary knowledge. However, the discipline–curriculum relationship is not linear, and school subjects, at all levels of schooling, differ in major ways from the disciplines they are intended to mirror. Elements taken from the disciplines are selected, and organised, framed, and translated—or converted—for specifically *educational* purposes.[127] These purposes vary according to the social, economic, and political context of the particular education system, but typically the aim is to develop certain skills and 'habits of mind' deemed important in the wider social context.[128] Traditionally, the discipline–curriculum relationship is loosely framed in the early years of schooling, but by senior secondary level it has tightened considerably, largely because there is a shift in the focus—and purposes—of schooling at this level. The early-years curriculum uses elements from the disciplines as contexts for building certain core skills in everyone, as the platform on which equal opportunity is, at least in theory, possible. The senior school

---

127 The framing idea comes from the work of the British educational sociologist Basil Bernstein (see, for example, Bernstein, 1971). The concept of curriculum development as translation comes from the work of the curriculum theorist Joseph Schwab (see, for example, Schwab, 1973), while 'conversion' was the term used by Jerome Bruner (see, for example, Bruner, 1966).
128 These could be dispositions or values (such as respect for others or fairness), or they could be orientations to thinking (such as investigating, analysing, or creating). Conventionally, they are an attempt to express the collective values and goals of the wider society at that point in time, and to set out a plan for reproducing them.

curriculum, on the other hand, is underpinned by a different ethos. There is a closer (but not direct) relationship between the subjects of the senior school curriculum and the university disciplines. This is because, in past years, the upper secondary school years were not compulsory. Their purpose was to screen students headed for university study from those who weren't, and to prepare students for study at this level. The curriculum at senior secondary level and the early-years curriculum thus have different *educational* purposes. This view of senior secondary education as having a different purpose—and therefore a different kind of curriculum—is, we think, part of Industrial Age thinking and no longer appropriate in the 21st century.

How, then, should we rethink the discipline–curriculum relationship for the 21st century? We think the key competencies concept in the new national curriculum document is a useful starting point. However, as things stand, the key competencies are likely to be ignored at senior secondary level because, as we have seen, the current national curriculum document is largely ignored after Year 10. In the current system, requiring schools to implement the new document and teach the key competencies in Years 11–13 is likely to be resisted and seen as yet another burden for already overworked teachers. Implementing a competencies-based senior secondary school curriculum requires us first to re-examine our ideas about what the senior secondary years are *for*, to look again at what we collectively expect of today's secondary school graduates, and at what individual students need in order to thrive in today's world.

So what *are* the key competencies? *Could* they be used to frame the curriculum at senior secondary level? How would this differ from the current system? How—and why—would this be an improvement?

The key competencies

The new national curriculum document identifies five key competencies that, it says, are used by people to:

> ... live, learn, work and contribute as active members of their communities. More complex than skills, the competencies draw also on knowledge, attitudes, and values in ways that lead to action. They are not separate or stand-alone. They are the *key to learning in every learning area*.[129] ... They are a focus for learning—and they enable learning.[130]

These key competencies are as follows:
1. managing self
2. relating to others
3. participating and contributing
4. thinking
5. using language, symbols, and text.

This emphasis on competencies is significant in that it represents the first steps in a move away from the old focus on knowledge-based credentials, to a new focus on developing certain broad areas of expertise or competencies. Competencies are not specific skills, but broad constellations of knowledge, skills, abilities, dispositions, and orientations that are built up over a long period of time. The five key competencies listed above can develop in many ways, in many contexts, but are seen as an essential foundation for thriving in the 21st century world. In this model, schooling's purpose is to scaffold the development of these competencies in everyone. As students move through the schooling system we should expect to see their competencies in these general areas broaden, deepen, and strengthen, and to see them develop an ability to apply these competencies in an increasing range of new and different contexts. All school leavers

---

129 Ministry of Education (2007), p. 12 (emphasis added).
130 Ministry of Education (2007), p. 38.

should be independent, self-directed thinkers and learners, in a wide range of different knowledge systems. They should be ready and willing to *go on* thinking and learning beyond school; they should be aware of their particular strengths (and weaknesses); and they should be able to work productively with people with different strengths and different backgrounds.

The foregrounding of competencies is a feature of recent developments across all sectors in New Zealand education.[131] Competencies appear in *Te Whāriki* (the national early childhood education curriculum document),[132] and in recent tertiary education policy documents,[133] as well as in the school curriculum. Some of these documents point out the alignment between each sector's (slightly different) competencies (see Figure 3 below).

Figure 3 Alignment of competency frameworks used in different education sectors[134]

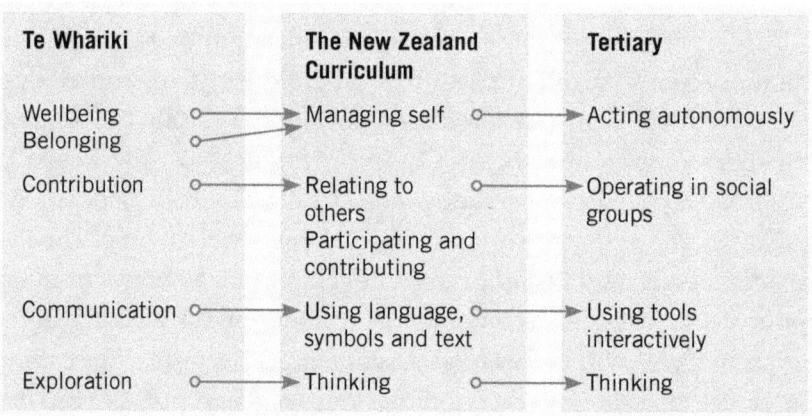

---

131 This work is part of, and influenced by, recent New Zealand and international research in this area; in particular, the OECD's DeSeCo (Defining and Selecting Competencies) project (OECD, 2000, 2002).
132 Ministry of Education (1996).
133 See, for example, Ministry of Education (2005).
134 Redrawn from the diagrams on p. 11 of Ministry of Education (2005) and p. 42 of Ministry of Education (2007).

The introduction of this cross-sectoral emphasis on competencies poses some significant challenges for the current senior secondary curriculum (and for some areas of the tertiary system). At the same time, however, we think it is important to point out that, although this approach to education will look very different on the surface, it is not actually all that different from the traditional approach. All the same elements—and general aims—are there. All that has happened is that the educational lens has been refocused in order to foreground—or make explicit—some things that in the old landscape tended to be in the background. This refocusing is, however, important. It is necessary if we want to make sure our young people get what they need to survive and thrive in the world of the future.

How is the competency-based model the same as the traditional subject-based approach? The traditional academic curriculum's core purpose, going right back to Plato, is to train the mind. Its goal is to build certain 'habits of mind', certain skills in thinking and reasoning that go beyond everyday or intuitive thinking. Students are not usually directly taught these habits of mind; rather, they are supposed to acquire them through the study of one or more of the traditional disciplines. Learning mathematics, science, history, or English literature teaches one to organise one's mind *as if one were* a mathematician, scientist, historian, or literary critic. After many years of study, a student can expect to understand the discipline: how one thinks in it, how new knowledge is developed in it, and how it 'works' overall, skills that are essential if one is to actually be a mathematician, scientist, and so on. However, the *educational* purpose in learning these things is *not* to produce apprentice mathematicians and so on: it is to develop certain important intellectual skills—the ability to think analytically, to synthesise, to think creatively and practically, and the ability to apply this thinking in a range of new and different situations.

Ironically, this core goal is often lost sight of. Teaching and assessment in the senior secondary school (and at early tertiary level) often focuses on the facts and details of a subject, as if learning these was somehow useful and important as an end in itself. This 'trainspotting' approach to knowledge is, for all but a very few students, not especially interesting or motivating. As a result, most students do not go on to really understand the subjects they study at the big-picture level (where it actually gets interesting), but, more importantly for the present purposes, they do not fully develop their higher order thinking skills. While, for all sorts of reasons, this was tolerated in the Industrial Age context, it cannot be justified in a 21st century education system. *Everyone* now needs the kind of higher order thinking skills formerly only developed at tertiary level, and they need to develop them by a more direct route than that allowed under the old apprenticeship model. Because people now need to go beyond understanding and reproducing existing knowledge, because they need the ability to work with knowledge to generate new knowledge, a 21st century education system needs to emphasise a systems-level understanding of knowledge, and higher order thinking skills.

These are the ideas behind key competencies 4 and 5 ('thinking' and 'using language, symbols and text'). Instead of, as in the past, focusing on filling up young people with bits of knowledge they might need in the world beyond school, and hoping that some of the thinking that produced that knowledge rubs off on them along the way, the new approach explicitly aims to develop those thinking skills, and the ability to use them in new and different contexts.

The key competencies framework also acknowledges that these skills, while very important, are not sufficient. To survive and thrive in the post-Industrial Age world, people will *also* need well-developed people and/or relationship skills, a high degree of self-awareness, and the kind of right-brain thinking skills outlined earlier. These ideas are the basis of key competencies 1, 2, and 3.

Thus the key competencies model reframes some of education's oldest and most important aims for the 21st century. The shift from 'knowing stuff' to 'doing stuff' allows us to think about learning, and about assessment, in new, post-Industrial Age ways. It is for this reason that we think this model could usefully be applied beyond Year 10 to the senior secondary curriculum. In the next section we look at how and why we need to think differently about learning and assessment.

Why do we need to think differently about learning?

Another important—and long-standing—educational goal is to build people's capacity to learn. While this idea is not new, terms like 'learning skills', 'learning how to learn' and 'lifelong learning' have in recent years become increasingly frequent in educational discussion. This trend is clearly part of the drive to reframe our education system for the 21st century. However, we have not, as yet, been especially successful in *actually* building people's capacity to learn.

One reason for this has to do with the dominance of the traditional disciplines (described above). Learning in the traditional context involves acquiring bits of knowledge and storing them away somewhere for future use (the 'gas tank' or 'empty vessel' model of education). At senior secondary level, because the system is designed to sort people according to their performance on tests designed to measure their mastery of this knowledge, the main future use of this knowledge is to be displayed in order to pass exams. In this context, the term 'learning skills' usually refers to various hints and tips on how to efficiently organise, retain, and retrieve information, and a successful learner is one who does well in exams. This approach does *not* build learning capacity and/or the ability to be a lifelong learner, and it is not a useful basis for a 21st century education system. As is well known, a great many students who do well in exams are not resilient, powerful, all-round learners (at least in part because teaching and learning for exam success do not foster these attributes, but actively select against them).[135] Conversely, many people who do poorly on school-type tests are highly effective learners in their out-of-school lives.

There are other reasons for our lack of success in designing educational approaches that genuinely build people's capacity to learn. As Guy Claxton points out, we have no clear conceptual framework for talking about what 'capacity to learn' involves; we have no coherent approach to pedagogy that focuses directly on expanding people's capacity to learn; and we have no reliable way of knowing when we have been successful. He argues for a shift away from 'learning skills' to an emphasis on what he calls 'learning dispositions'.[136] A skill is the ability to do something, usually something specific that can be described and known in advance (by someone else). Having a skill does not mean that we want to use it, that we know when and where to use it, or that we recognise its relevance in new situations. Learning a skill is part of being trained to do specific things: it is not necessarily a useful part of being *educated*; that is, becoming an independent thinker and learner. A disposition, on the other hand, is an ability that one is actually disposed—that is, ready and willing—to make use of. One can know *how* to 'be questioning' for example. One can know how to formulate good questions and how to tell one type of question from another. But the *disposition* to be questioning requires one to *want*—and to have the self-confidence—to ask questions, and to not mind risking that everyone else knows the answer to one's question. It also means that

---

[135] See, for example, the work on 'bright girls' and mathematics achievement reported in Dweck (2000).
[136] See Claxton (2007).

one will *go on* asking questions, even when no longer supported and encouraged to do so, and in new and different contexts.

As Claxton argues, teaching young people to be disposed to learning, as opposed to teaching them learning skills, requires a significant culture change in schools. It requires a different orientation, different kinds of activities, a different language, and different forms of assessment. It requires us to put learning in the foreground and knowledge acquisition in the background. It also requires us to abandon the traditional stories teachers (and parents) use to motivate young people. This, we think, is a crucial part of the culture change, one that is a necessary prerequisite to building a 21st century education system, and that also allows us to avoid some of the unproductive blind alleys we have found ourselves in recently (e.g., the recent debate over the future direction of the NCEA).

New motivational stories

The idea of the senior school examination system as a key hurdle—or initiation rite—of adolescence is so deeply embedded in our culture that it is very hard to think outside it. Passing—or, as we now say, 'achieving'—the milestone of NCEA, or, for the previous generation, School Certificate, has a symbolic function that goes way beyond the apparent purpose of these tests of a student's ability to demonstrate that they know—or can do—certain highly prescribed things. Success in these tests provides access to a range of different social and economic opportunities, while failure closes them down—or so the story goes. We motivate students to study hard by telling them that if they get good grades and good qualifications, they will get a good job and be happy. We also use this story to attempt to control and discipline boisterous and distracted adolescents (with varying degrees of success).

This story is not necessarily true,[137] and it is not especially motivating for young people.[138] However, and importantly for the present purposes, it is quite unproductive if our goal is to build students' long-term capacity for learning. Encouraging young people to remember and/or do certain things in order to pass a test so that they can accumulate NCEA credits is, we think, to miss the point of what they are at school *for*. It is certainly not an adequate basis for preparing them for 21st century life and work. If young people are to become powerful, resilient, long-term learners they have to be willing—that is, internally motivated—to be stretched and challenged. They will have to work hard and, importantly, they will have to understand why they should do this. Being chivvied and/or disciplined by teachers (and parents) will not build the kind of learning dispositions they need to thrive in the world of the future. Clearly we need new stories to motivate young people, and to allow teachers to rethink their role in all this.

One possibility is Claxton's 'learning gym' idea.[139] If the aim of schools is to develop 'fitter minds', then getting mentally 'fitter' involves being stretched and getting tired. The exertion is tolerable, pleasurable even, because it gets you where you want to go. Teachers,

---

137 Although there are general statistical relationships between education, income, and general health, this of course does not mean that higher levels of education *cause* higher levels in these other things: rather these things tend to go together in particular social groups. It also does not mean that this pattern follows for all individuals. As is well known, plenty of people who leave school with few or no formal qualifications are highly successful in the world beyond school. In addition, because it is based on a qualification system in which the 'value' of the qualifications lies in their scarcity, clearly not everyone who works hard will get good grades and the qualification. The qualifications 'game' depends on only *some* students being successful, even in competency-based systems.

138 It is interesting that, in the current discussions of the apparently demotivating effects of the NCEA, the primary concern is for students who, because they would have done well under the old system, could be seen as 'losing out' in the new system.

139 See Claxton (1999, 2002, 2004).

in this model, are 'learning coaches'. They help students develop suitable learning programmes and support them at first, but the eventual aim is to have students develop their own programmes. According to Claxton, if we are to recruit young people's energy for—and commitment to—their own education, we need to explain:

> ... that school isn't really about the Tudors and the Periodic Table. It is about becoming a brave and skilled explorer; a cunning detective; an imaginative creator; a tough competitor—in whatever field of life they want to work and play in. We have to talk to them seriously about what we are up to; what they can expect to gain; and what they will have to put in.[140]

Claxton goes on to quote a 14-year-old participant in a research project's story about why he goes to school:

> Why do I come to school? To develop my learning power of course! They give us interesting things to explore that get harder and harder. In finding out how to grapple with them, we develop the 'learning muscles' and learning stamina that will enable us to get better at whatever we want, for the rest of our lives. People like scientists and historians have figured out special purpose ways to learn: as we get older we practice [sic] those, and think about how they might help us in everyday life. As powerful learners, we will be better able to learn new skills, solve new problems, have new ideas and make new friends. We know that learning itself is the one ability that will never go out of date—guaranteed—(unlike programming your iPod). And no matter how so-called 'bright' you are, everyone can get better at learning. Even professors have learning difficulties! Oh, and by the way, as we become more powerful learners, so we naturally do better on examinations too! It's a no-brainer really. (Kyle, 14, Cardiff)[141]

Claxton's conclusion is that education's most important task today is:

> ... trying to find a form of schooling that enables all young people to get better at learning—to come at life venturesome, imaginative and

---

140 Claxton (2007), p. 131.
141 Claxton (2007), p. 132.

questioning. ... [T]rying to find a way of presenting and explaining this, so that youngsters see the point and are willing, in much greater numbers, to put in some effort and give it a go, is the most urgent bit of PR that our society requires.[142]

These new 'stories' will need to be accompanied by some rethinking of the way we organise secondary education. The next section looks at how we might begin to do this.

New metaphors

Reorienting the senior secondary school towards this learning-centred, competency-based approach requires some organisational changes.

Currently, senior secondary education is structured like a river that splits off into two branches. Students are channelled into one of two main pathways from school: the tertiary and/or further—education pathway, or the vocational training and/or direct entry to work pathway. After completing Years 9 and 10, students navigate their way through the river (around rocks, submerged trees, and other obstacles), choosing which stream to follow (via their subject choices). They gradually steer themselves—or are steered—into position to take one of two forks in the river.

The senior school qualifications are like the final set of rapids before the two forks diverge from one another. Depending on which subjects students take, their senior qualifications will either allow them to take a course through the academic rapids and into tertiary education, or through the vocational rapids into a different kind of post-school pathway.

The academic rapids represent the qualifications required for university entry—usually some sort of score calculated from students' achievement in a specified set of approved subjects. (Students' marks in other, non approved, subjects are not counted

---

142 *Ibid.*

Metaphor 1: A forked river

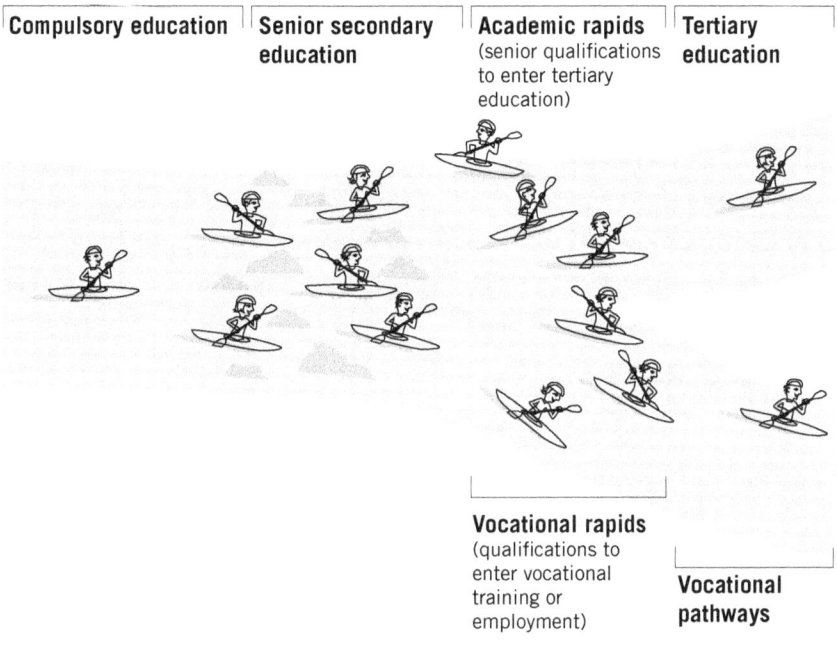

in the calculation of their tertiary entrance score, although they do count towards their overall senior secondary qualification.)

If a student has been heading towards one fork of the river but decides they want to change to another, this can be difficult (though not impossible). Paddling sideways across rivers is difficult, as is paddling backwards out of rapids. However, they can haul their kayak out of the river and drag it backwards, restarting at a point in the river that will take them to their new chosen fork. This will of course delay their progress overall. Alternatively, if they have already gone some way down one fork, they can haul out and clamber overland to negotiate their way into the other stream as an adult student.

As outlined in Part 1 of this book, the traditional model of senior secondary education represented in this metaphor is now under pressure. Among other things, it was not set up to meet the needs of the very diverse group of students that now move through it. Are there ways we could play with this metaphor, adapting it to allow the river to better support young people as they make their way along it? In what follows we put forward some ideas for doing this. One possibility is to adapt the forked river idea to allow more flexibility and easier transfer between the different pathways. Instead of dividing into two distinct branches after Year 10, the secondary education river could 'braid' into a number of different channels or streams that separate from each other and then merge back together.

Metaphor 2: A braided river

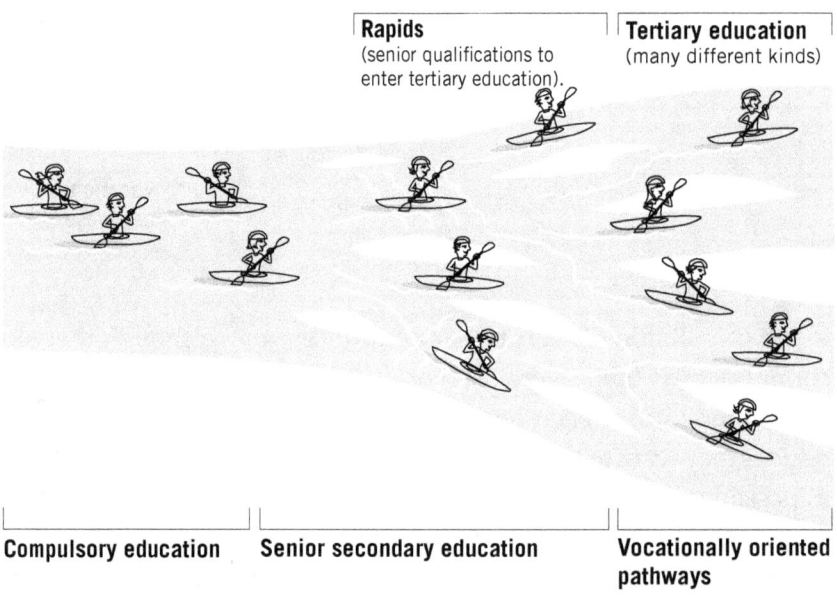

This metaphor acknowledges that people will take different pathways when they leave school, but the 'rapids' (i.e., qualification structures) are organised so that people's options are not closed down early by early subject choices, and to allow people to change courses. Students can follow their interests, but also change their minds and work towards a different post-school pathway, all the while continuing to move down the secondary school river. They can mix academic and vocational learning throughout their secondary education, whatever they think they will do after secondary school.[143]

Our third metaphor is similar to the braided river one, but it adds in a stop-off point—or safe haven—for students who are having trouble navigating or even staying afloat. These could be students with learning difficulties, or students with other difficulties in their lives that have meant that school has either not been a priority or has not met their needs. To avoid allowing these students to drown, or be washed up on an uninhabited part of the riverbank, a camping ground area is set up to give these students a different, non-'mainstream' senior secondary experience, the eventual aim being that they have the skills and confidence to go back into the river. The camping ground teachers would be more like mentors and the students could spend time learning together as a group, mixing work experience learning with programmes designed to develop life skills, personal development skills, and the educational basics (e.g., literacy and numeracy).[144]

Metaphors 1, 2, and 3 maintain the traditional screening and sorting function of senior secondary education, albeit, in the case of Metaphors 2 and 3, in ways that genuinely attempt to better meet the needs of all students. With minimal disturbance to the traditional

---

143 The Queensland education system is moving in this direction. There, all students who complete senior secondary school are awarded a senior certificate, but the certificates differ depending on the subjects they took. All students also sit a test of 'core skills', which is like a 'rapid' that everybody traverses whatever they are doing/learning in senior secondary school. The NCEA could potentially be used to do this, if we could identify and agree on some core competencies.

144 The senior secondary systems in Victoria and in Ireland have this kind of camping ground structure. In both systems there are questions and issues. For example, is it desirable to separate these students off in ways that are likely to limit their future options? Alternatively, aren't there aspects of these programmes that all students would benefit from—like the focus on learning work skills, working and learning together in teams, different student–teacher relationships, and so on?

Metaphor 3: Braided river with a camping ground for 'drowning' students

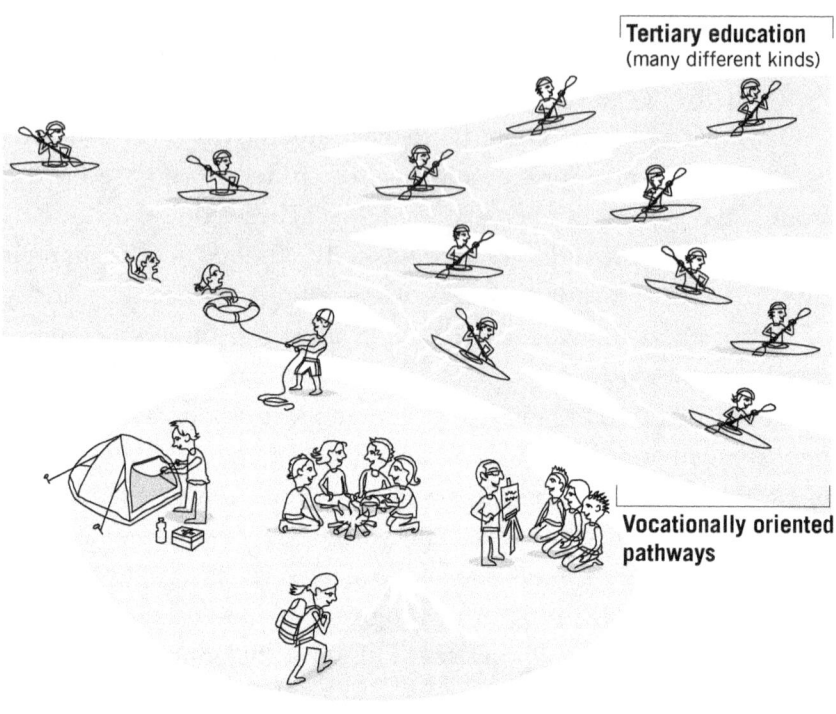

university-bound pathway, they broaden the choices and pathways available to those not heading to university, and provide more support for students who are struggling. The traditional secondary subjects are maintained, as is the traditional notion of senior secondary assessment as a key adolescent rite of passage. Metaphors 1, 2, and 3 do not, we think, allow us to make the shift to the 21st century educational aim of building everyone's capacity to learn. Can the river metaphor be adapted to allow us to make this shift? Metaphor 4 below is a first, rather imperfect, attempt to do this.

Metaphor 4: A networked camping ground

Students could meet in a central 'camping ground' (the school site) with their teacher/mentors to plan their learning programmes. The camping ground could have several different 'loop tracks' that lead to a variety of different learning experiences.[145] Some of these could resemble traditional work experience programmes (working with, for example, a mechanic, a veterinarian, a film-maker, or a hairdresser for a specified period of time); or they could involve researching (perhaps by interviewing people) the skills and knowledge required for these jobs. Other experiences could involve designing, setting up, and carrying out a research project that investigates and recommends solutions to a real local issue or problem. Others could involve writing, designing, and performing a play, a musical performance, or an art exhibition.

The point of these experiences is *not* for students to learn how a mechanic spends their day, how to write a submission to a local council, or how to put on a play (although this would of course happen—and be a good thing). The purpose of these experiences, together with others, is to provide contexts which will develop students' overall capacity to learn: to do things with knowledge, to be curious and questioning, to think and learn independently, and to evaluate—and improve—their own thinking and learning.

The camping ground needs to be located in or near to—and, importantly, to be *part of*—a 'real world' community or village, because the village/community's resources and issues are the

---

[145] The Welsh Baccalaureate Qualification is one example of an attempt to realise this idea. It has a core curriculum that all 16–19-year-olds take, irrespective of the other options they may have chosen. This core emphasises not the traditional subjects, but certain essential skills (including communication, number, and IT skills; improving one's own learning; working with others, for an employer, and in a local community; enterprise skills and problem solving); as well as knowledge of Wales and its relationship with the rest of the world. Students are supported by well-developed pastoral/guidance and tutorial systems. (See http://www.wbq.org.uk, or National Assembly for Wales (2003) for details.)

students' learning resources and, conversely, the students' knowledge-generation activities should be a resource for the community.

Metaphor 4: A networked camping ground

21st century work and learning possibilities

The role of the camping ground teachers is *not* to be the source of all the knowledge the students need, but to act as learning coaches. They mentor students as they work out which loop tracks to go on, in which order. They help students plan what they need to know before starting each track, and what they need to take. They also connect students with useful information sources—people, websites, databases, or books, and with possible collaborators; provide the infrastructure students need to complete each track successfully; and provide opportunities for them to report on their findings when they return.

The camping ground teachers also work with students over time to help them plan the development of their 'portfolio' of learning, and with other teachers to develop school-wide plans for ensuring—and assessing—that all students *are* building their learning capacity. The goal is to support students to carry out their own needs assessment, and to organise, direct, and generate their own learning; that is, to invent, design, and coproduce themselves as learners.

In this model the teacher–student relationship is not an expert–novice one, but a collaboration. New knowledge is developed in, and because of, this collaboration by *both* participants. Teaching and learning are to some extent merged (as in the Māori concept of ako). This does not, of course, mean that teachers' knowledge doesn't matter, or that teachers do not need to know anything. Teachers will have to know a great deal, ideally about a wide range of different subject areas, to do this effectively. However, this knowledge, while necessary, will not be sufficient. Just as in the present system teachers need to be able to interpret the one-size-fits-all curriculum in ways that engage and work for all their students, in a personalised system teachers will need to be able to engage each and every student in a discussion of how best to go about building the student's personal learning capacity. Doing this effectively requires significant background subject knowledge, a good understanding of different learning theories, and significant expertise in working effectively with young people. For this to work, teachers and students have to expect—and want—to get something out of this partnership, and they have to respect, value, and be ready to hear the contributions of the other partner. This personalised model of learning obviously requires a fairly major culture shift. However, it is, we think, a very good way of allowing us to think outside some of the unhelpful structures of the past, while at the same time maintaining a commitment to education's traditional—and core—goals.

By now you might be wondering what happened to the river in this metaphor. In Metaphors 1, 2, and 3 the river was central. However, in Metaphor 4 its importance is greatly reduced. Its only role really is to bring students to the camping ground, and maybe carry them away later, when they are ready to move into the world beyond school. In Metaphors 1, 2, and 3 the river represents 'the system': a one-size/one-speed-for-all system that students must fit into and keep up with. While there are some supports, students must participate in this system if they want to 'get anywhere'. Those who don't, drown, or are cast ashore without the skills and knowledge they need in the river's lower reaches. Metaphor 4 represents a more personalised approach to learning in which it is possible to get somewhere by a variety of different routes, at a speed that suits the individual. Because, in the 21st century, we are less sure that we know exactly where that somewhere is (and what it looks like), we can no longer be so sharply focused on the one best way. Metaphor 4 thus refocuses the traditional educational landscape. The river/system moves into the background, as do the old hurdles and the old emphasis on subjects. Lifting everyone's game is in the foreground. The central goal is to develop certain key competencies in *everyone*, to use—and build on—people's strengths and interests, while also ensuring that everyone has the basics, via a system that allows people to follow personalised learning pathways.

The personalised learning idea has been much discussed recently, in various initiatives in the UK and then, in modified form, here in New Zealand. We think this idea has a great deal of potential to scaffold our thinking as we redevelop our education system for the 21st century. However, there are some pitfalls, some traps we could fall into if we try to make this idea fit within existing structures. In the final section of this book we explore how we might make this idea work for a 21st century education system.

Personalising learning: basic tenet of 21st century education, or yet another burden for teachers?

What *is* personalising learning? At its most basic, personalising learning just means tailoring educational programmes to individual students' needs, interests, and aptitudes. It means designing educational programmes that put *students* at the centre, rather than making students fit the system.[146] According to the UK Futurelab group:

> ... the logic of education systems should be reversed so that it is the system that conforms to the learner, rather than the learner to the system. This is the essence of personalisation. It demands a system capable of offering bespoke support for each individual that recognises and builds upon their diverse strengths, interests, abilities and needs in order to foster engaged and independent learners able to reach their full potential.[147]

In 2006/07 the personalising learning concept was taken up by Steve Maharey when he was New Zealand's Minister of Education.[148] As he saw it, the concept is a useful way of drawing together 'all the great things that are happening to prepare our kids for a knowledge society and for life-long learning',[149] and developing a 21st century version of the 'Beeby vision' for New Zealand education.[150] It can address six important goals:

1. improving equity: finding a new way to overcome the uneven results of New Zealand's education system, moving it from a high-

---

146 See, for example, DfES (2004); Leadbeater (2004, 2005); Miliband (2004, 2006); Centre for Educational Research and Innovation (2006); Campbell, Robinson, Neelands, Hewston, & Mazzoli (2007).
147 Green, Facer, Rudd, Dillon & Humphreys (2006).
148 See the booklet *Let's Talk About Personalizing Learning* (Ministry of Education, 2006a).
149 See Maharey (2007).
150 This term is widely used to refer to the text of a speech, written by Dr C. E. Beeby (Director-General of Education at the time), but given by Peter Fraser, the Minister of Education in New Zealand's first Labour Government, in 1939. The part of the speech that is usually quoted is as follows: "The Government's objective, broadly expressed, is that every person, whatever his level of academic ability, whether he be rich or poor, whether he live in town or country, has a right, as a citizen, to a free education of the kind for which he is best fitted, and to the fullest extent of his powers. So far is this from being a mere pious platitude that the full acceptance of the principle will involve the reorientation of the education system" (Fraser, P., *AJHR* 1939, pp. 2–3, quoted in Beeby, 1986).

excellence, low-equity system to a high-excellence, high-equity system
2. improving student motivation or engagement in learning: finding new ways to hook 'digital age learners' into learning
3. shifting away from the old ways of thinking about learning (students passively receive knowledge) to a view of learners as actively engaged—with their teachers and others—in a dynamic, two-way process of co-constructing knowledge
4. providing opportunities for students (at all levels) to get some of their needs met outside traditional classrooms and age-related cohorts—outside schools even, thus expanding the range of learning options available to them
5. providing for a student voice in choosing what, how, and why they might want to learn
6. achieving a better articulation between education and other public services and between education and the world of work (the education system is currently lagging behind—not leading—the transition to the Knowledge Society).[151]

None of these goals are especially new. Achieving equity and tailoring education to individual needs and interests have long been ideals, but for reasons outlined earlier in this book they are ideas that have proved to be very difficult to implement in a generalised way across the system. Personalising learning is a concept that could very easily become just another educational buzzword, regularly uttered but not always understood, conflated with other concepts—mixed-ability teaching, or individual education programmes (IEPs), for example—or written off as implying that 'anything goes' and 'nothing matters'. We think that this is highly likely unless we think very carefully about *how* and *why*—if at all—it should be implemented.

---

151 Gilbert (2007); Gilbert & Bolstad (2006); see also Humphreys (2006).

One of its strengths as a unifying concept is that it seems simple and familiar. However, this is also a weakness. It will be tempting to see personalising learning as the answer to the question of how to address the above goals *within the existing system*. This would be a very bad idea: firstly, it won't work; and secondly, it *won't* transform the education system for the Knowledge Society. What then should we do?

We think the personalising learning concept is best seen as a way of *linking* familiar ideas about best practice in education with new ideas about how education could be transformed for the 21st century. Figure 4 below is an attempt to represent this idea.

Figure 4 Two worlds of thought that underpin and link to the concept of personalising learning

PERSONALISED LEARNING

'Simple/familiar' interpretations: Linked to past and current policy and practice. Current and evidence-based ideas about good teaching practice (e.g., tailoring learning to individual need and interest). Identifying the best examples of current practice and generalising this to makesure that all students experience the best possible learning and teaching.

'Complex/transformative' interpretations: Linked to current and future policy and practice. New ideas about how education (and other public services) will need to be reshaped for the 21st century and beyond. Creating a new educational 'myth' to underpin the design of a system that supports 21st century learning/lifelong learning.

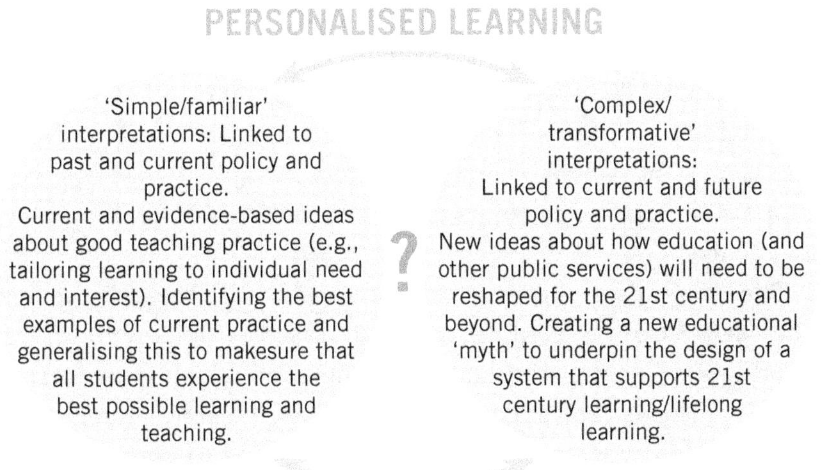

This representation is designed to focus attention on the space *between* these two 'worlds of thought', on the—possibly highly productive—*interactions* that could take place in this space.[152]

---

152 See Gilbert & Bolstad (2006).

How, then, could ideas from 'world one' be put together with those from 'world two' in a way that is easy to understand *and* is transformative? What different forms could the personalising learning concept take, and what effect would each have if implemented? We think there are three broad possibilities, each of which is a different balance of ideas from world one and world two.[153] These three models are as follows.

Model 1: Mass customisation—extrapolating and refining the status quo

In this model, personalising learning is simply added to the status quo without disturbing current aims and objectives. Efforts are made to allow more flexible pathways through the system, to allow multilevel study and the development of modular approaches. There is a certain amount of choice for students as they assemble customised packages of modules to build 'portfolios of learning'. The system provides a better (that is, more personalised) 'service' to its 'customers' (learners) than now, but the system and its suppliers still define the options. Teachers are no longer the conduits for all knowledge, but act as 'learning brokers', people whose role is to support and advise students as they develop their learning plans and goals.

The system's customers are, however, still largely passive. They select from a fixed set of standardised options with limited information (mostly supplied by teachers) on which to make their choices. (This is rather like Dell Computer's current strategy: Dell offers to build you a new computer customised to your particular needs, as defined through a conversation with the salesperson about how you want to use the computer.) The system's customers wait for suppliers to design, develop, and provide new learning modules. Suppliers develop new modules on an as-and-when-required basis,

---

153 These three models are based on ideas drawn from the following sources: Bentley & Miller (2006); Leadbeater (2004, 2006); Miller & Bentley (2003).

but they are usually constructed by repackaging existing materials, derived from the traditional subjects. However, a bigger catalogue of products is available to the customers/learners. The supplier assesses customer performance according to the modules selected, and performance/quality standards still mainly focus on what learners know after they have completed the module.

Thus the relationship between the 'producers' of educational products and services and the 'consumers' of these products and services remains largely as it is now—supplier/producer driven. Learning modules are mass-produced and standardised. They use mainly current curriculum materials, current ideas about pedagogy, and current assessment methods. The capacity of the consumer/demand side to articulate or refine its needs (beyond the very basic) is not well developed, and the system has nothing in place to develop this capacity. On the other hand, the work can be completed in many different ways, and learners can work at different levels in different areas.

This approach is basically a modified version of the status quo. It is *not* transformative, because it uses existing curriculum, pedagogy, and methods of assessment; it doesn't alter existing institutional structures; it doesn't require any change in the roles of teachers and students; and it doesn't question the underlying assumptions that produce these things as they are now. It relies on the old methods of production and consumption, the old methods of knowledge management (hierarchical, disciplinary, 'command and control'), and the old understanding of knowledge. It does *not* meet the needs of the knowledge-based societies of the future, and it does not provide a space from which the education system can be innovative. It could actually slow change. On the other hand it does move in the direction of limited customisation, and it would probably produce more knowledge-intensive, evidence-based approaches to education in schools. It is a mass-produced, limited way of customising a basically uncritiqued model of learning. (It is, however, more or less the approach that is currently being adopted in the UK.)

Model 2: Diverse suppliers—extending the market model

This model is similar to the above (in that it offers mass customisation, greater flexibility, multiple pathways, more student choice, and so on), but it differs in that it allows a range of different suppliers (not necessarily public schools) to compete to deliver educational services (modules of learning, for example). The underlying premise is that student choice and competition between suppliers will push up the overall quality of these products and services.

Learners/customers build their learning programme by choosing from a range of options, depending on their needs as they (or their parents/carers) see them. However, these options basically involve mixing and matching standardised components (again, rather like the Dell Computer example outlined above). A bigger catalogue of products would be available, and there would be more flexible delivery of those products. However, the market would continue to be supplier driven, and public education would be like a shopping mall. In this model, consumers are the passive recipients of educational services designed by others for a mass market. As in Model 1 above, the system is not required to support consumers to take a more active and informed role in the development of products designed to meet their needs.

This approach allows education to break out of the top-down, command and control management styles of the Industrial Age, but at the same time it allows the larger or public-good goals of public education to recede into the background. Quality is reduced to consumer flexibility and/or consumer preference. As in Model 1, consumers will, in most cases, not have sufficient information to make genuinely informed choices. Some consumer groups will very definitely be advantaged over others, and education's equity goal will be threatened. This model is not especially innovative and it doesn't meet the needs of the Knowledge Society. Like Model 1 above, it involves a fairly superficial customising of a basically uncritiqued model of learning.

Model 3: Joining up supply and demand—developing 'prosumers'

This model allows the education system to think outside the square of existing models of curriculum, pedagogy, and assessment. Students actively co-construct their own 'catalogue' or 'menu' of products *and* design the products. With informed help from older, more knowledgeable others (usually education professionals), students carry out a needs assessment for themselves and, using this, conceive and design their own programme of learning. A key role of the adult education professional is to help the learner connect with a range of information sources, suppliers, and possible collaborators (these could be local, or on the other side of the world). However, the process is user organised, directed, and generated. Learners are thus actively involved, not only in their own learning, but also in developing the capacity to invent, design, and co-produce themselves (many young people are doing this already—via websites like *MySpace, FaceBook,* and *YouTube* and through games like *The Sims*). Key to this model is the joining-up relationship, the collaboration between supplier and consumer. This relationship is central. It is mutually beneficial, symbiotic even, to the extent that the partners could be reconceived as 'prosumers'.

In this model, learning is not something done to the specification of another (or of a system), but something that is motivated by its personalisation. Put another way, this model does not involve personalising learning (as we now know it); rather, learning *is personalisation*. Young people design, invent, and produce themselves as learners who are individuals *and* part of collectivities. These collectivities, important in terms of the continued legitimacy of public education, can shift, change, and re-form for different purposes.

Developing this model obviously requires learners to change the 'script' they have for themselves in relation to education. It also requires educational professionals to change their script and, importantly, it requires a system-wide change in the national educational script. Changing these scripts creates the spaces within which innovation can be produced.[154]

This model *could* be transformative. It could deal with the new view of knowledge, and it could stimulate the kinds of changes needed if we are to build a genuinely future-focused education system. It does *not* involve giving up the public-good goals of a public education system, as is likely with the diverse-suppliers model. It could improve the productivity of the system (raising overall levels of achievement), and improve equity (although this would involve developing new, postmodern conceptions of equity that do not involve sameness).[155] The hard part, though, is that it requires us to actively imagine—and create—the future, to do more than just identify and follow trends. It requires us to imagine new pedagogies, new curricula, and new forms of assessment. It requires us to imagine new roles for teachers, and new roles for 'the system'.

The way ahead?

In this chapter we have argued that many of the ideas that drive the current senior secondary curriculum are making it very difficult for us to develop a 21st century curriculum. We have made the case for replacing the traditional subject-oriented model, which encourages students to master specific bits of knowledge to pass exams and accumulate credits for qualifications, with a competency-oriented model that supports students to develop personalised programmes designed to build overall learning capacity.

---

154 The 'script' concept, and the idea that changes in scripts allow innovation comes from Leadbeater (2004). This point is similar to the 'new stories' idea outlined earlier in this section.
155 See Chapter 5 of Gilbert (2005) for an explanation of this idea.

We think this is important because in the 21st century we do not know what the future is. We can't specify in advance the kinds of finished product knowledge and skills students need for successful and happy lives. Therefore we need to ensure that all young people leave school with the kind of raw materials or competencies that allow them to respond to almost anything. To use a biological metaphor, our schools are currently set up to produce clones: conformist, rule-following copies of ourselves who faithfully reproduce what is given to them. Biologically speaking, a clone is an exact copy of the parent organism which can only function successfully in the environment for which it is specialised: it has no means of adapting to a new environment. Clones are thus evolutionary dead ends. 'Clades', on the other hand, are unspecialised organisms that colonise the new environments created when there is a change to the 'balance of nature'. Their offspring diversify and specialise to form a whole variety of new species. A clade is thus the opposite of a clone: it has within it the capacity to develop in any one of a number of different directions, and it is the foundation of great leaps forward in evolution. Clades represent diversity, dynamism, innovation, and ongoing life, while clones signify conformity, constriction, and eventual death.[156] Industrial Age societies needed clones, but in the 21st century, the Industrial Age 'balance of nature' has been disrupted. If the products of our schools are to flourish in this new environment, they need the capacity to develop in a variety of different directions and, importantly, the capacity to decide for themselves which direction to follow. Many of the elements of traditional secondary education are explicitly designed to produce clones, not clades. If we are to refocus secondary education for the 21st century, we need to reconfigure these elements to allow us to achieve education's traditional core aim—producing independent, self-directed, lifelong learners—in new ways. The purpose of this book has been to provoke what we hope will be an ongoing discussion of how we might do this.

---

156 The clade metaphor is used in Beare (2001), following Dyson (1981).

References

Allison, J. (2005). *Issues around the senior curriculum*. Paper presented to the Curriculum/Marautanga Project meeting, Wellington, 11 May 2007.

Beare, H. (2001). *Creating the future school*. London: Routledge.

Beare, H., & Slaughter, R. (1993). *Education for the twenty-first century*. London: Routledge.

Beeby, C. (1986). Introduction. In W. Renwick (Ed.), *Moving targets: Six essays on educational policy* (pp. xi–xlv). Wellington: New Zealand Council for Educational Research.

Bell, B., Jones, A., & Carr, M. (1995). The development of the recent national New Zealand science curriculum. *SAMEPapers 1995*, pp. 3–44.

Bentley, T., & Miller, R. (2006). Personalisation: Getting the questions right. In Centre for Educational Research and Innovation, *Schooling for tomorrow: Personalising education* (pp. 115–126). Paris: OECD.

Bereiter, C. (2002). *Education and mind in the Knowledge Age*. Mahwah, NJ: Lawrence Erlbaum Associates.

Bernstein, B. (1971). On the classification and framing of educational knowledge. In M. Young (Ed.), *Knowledge and control: New directions in the sociology of education* (pp. 47–69). London: Collier Macmillan.

Bigum, C. (2003). The knowledge-producing school: Moving away from the work of finding educational problems for which computers are the solution. *Computers in New Zealand Schools*, 15(2), 22–26.

Bolstad, R. (2004). *School-based curriculum development: Principles, processes, and practices*. Wellington: New Zealand Council for Educational Research.

Boreham, N. (2002). Work process knowledge, curriculum control and the work-based route to vocational qualifications. *British Journal of Educational Studies*, 59(2), 225–237.

Boyd, S., McDowall, S., & Cooper, G. (2002). *Innovative pathways from school—the case studies: Phase One report 2002*. Wellington: New Zealand Council for Educational Research.

Brewerton, M. (2004). *Thoughts on what students need to learn at school: Summary for discussion purposes*. Paper prepared for the Ministry of Education. Retrieved 12 September, 2006, from http://www.tki.org.nz/e/tki/

Bruner, J. (1966). *Towards a theory of instruction*. Cambridge, MA: Harvard University Press.

Butterworth, G., & Butterworth, S. (1998). *Reforming education: The New Zealand experience 1984–1996*. Palmerston North: Dunmore Press.

Campbell, R., Robinson, W., Neelands, J., Hewston, R., & Mazzoli, L. (2007). Personalised learning: Ambiguities in theory and practice. *British Journal of Educational Studies*, 55(2), 135–154.

Castells, M. (2000). *The rise of the network society* (2nd ed.). Oxford: Blackwell.

Centre for Educational Research and Innovation. (2006). *Schooling for tomorrow: Personalising education*. Paris: OECD.

Claxton, G. (1999). *Wise up: Learning to live the learning life*. London: Bloomsbury.

Claxton, G. (2002). *Building learning power: How to help young people become better learners*. Bristol, UK: TLO.

Claxton, G. (2004). Mathematics and the mind gym: How subject teaching develops a learning mentality. *For the Learning of Mathematics*, 24(2), 27–32.

Claxton, G. (2007). Expanding young people's capacity to learn. *British Journal of Educational Studies, 55*(2), 115–134.

Cook, L. (2000). *Looking past the 20th century: A selection of long-term statistical trends that influence and shape public policy in New Zealand*. Wellington: Statistics New Zealand. Retrieved 18 May 2005, from http://www.stats.govt.nz/looking-past-20th-century/default.htm

Department for Education and Skills. (2004). *A national conversation about personalised learning*. Nottingham, UK: Author. Retrieved 11 August 2006, from http://www.standards.dfes.gov.uk/personalisedlearning

Department of Education. (1944). *The post-primary school curriculum: Report of the committee appointed by the Minister of Education in November 1942*. Wellington: Author.

Department of Education. (1988). *Tomorrow's Schools: The reform of education administration in New Zealand*. Wellington: Author.

Durie, M. (2006, September). *Students first: Implications, consequences and outcomes*. Keynote address to the Marking a Future Path symposium (Secondary Futures Project), Wellington.

Dweck, C. (2000). *Self-theories*. Hove, UK: Psychology Press.

Dwyer, P. (1995). Pathways in post-compulsory education: From metaphor to practice. *Australian Journal of Education, 39*(2), 146–162.

Dyson, F. (1981). *Disturbing the universe*. London: Pan.

Elley, W. (2003, 19 February). New assessment system does not pass test. *New Zealand Education Review*, pp. 5–6.

Elley, W. (2005). *Facts and fallacies about standards-based assessment*. Address to Macleans College, Auckland. Retrieved 19 August, 2007, from http://www.macleans.school.nz/news/pages/2005/pdfs/warwickelley/address.pdf

Elley, W., Hall, C., & Marsh, R. (2004). Rescuing NCEA: Some possible ways forward. *New Zealand Annual Review of Education, 14*, 5–25.

Fiske, E., & Ladd, H. (2000). *When schools compete: A cautionary tale*. Washington, DC: Brookings Institute.

Friedman, T. (2006). *The world is flat: A brief history of the twenty-first century*. Camberwell, Vic: Penguin.

Gardner, H. (2006). *Five minds for the future*. Boston, MA: Harvard Business School Press.

Gilbert, J. (2005). *Catching the Knowledge Wave?: The Knowledge Society and the future of education*. Wellington: NZCER Press.

Gilbert, J. (2007). *Personalising learning: Discussion paper for the Ministry of Education*. Unpublished paper.

Gilbert, J., & Bolstad, R. (2006). *Personalising learning: A background paper for the Ministry of Education*. Unpublished paper.

Green, H., Facer, K., & Rudd, T., with Dillon, P., & Humphreys, P. (2006). *Personalisation and digital technologies: Futurelab*. Retrieved 30 August 2006, from www.futurelab.org.uk/research/personalisation.htm

Growth and Innovation Advisory Board. (2005). *Creating successful school leavers: What businesses of the future will need from school leavers of the future*. Wellington: Think Tank Consulting.

Hall, C. (1999). National Certificate of Educational Achievement: Issues of reliability, validity and manageability. *New Zealand Annual Review of Education, 9*, 173–192.

Hipkins, R. (2007). *Course innovation in the senior secondary curriculum: A snapshot taken in July 2007*. Wellington: New Zealand Council for Educational Research.

Hipkins, R., Conner, L., & Neill, A. (2006). *Shifting balances 2: The impact of Level One and Two NCEA implementation on the teaching of geography and home economics*. Wellington: Ministry of Education.

Hipkins, R., & Vaughan, K. (2002). *From cabbages to kings: interim research report—first year of learning curves: Meeting student learning needs in an evolving qualifications regime*. Wellington: New Zealand Council for Educational Research.

Hipkins, R., Vaughan, K., Beals, F., & Ferral, H. (2004). *Learning curves: Meeting student learning needs in an evolving qualifications regime—shared pathways and multiple tracks: A second report*. Wellington: New Zealand Council for Educational Research.

Hipkins, R., & Vaughan, K., with Beals, F., Ferral, H., & Gardiner, B. (2005). *Shaping our futures: meeting secondary students' learning needs in a time of evolving qualifications final report for the Learning Curves project*. Wellington: New Zealand Council for Educational Research.

Horrocks, R., & Hoben, N. (2005). *Media studies and English in the new curriculum*. Unpublished paper prepared for the Ministry of Education/New Zealand Curriculum/Marautanga project.

Humphreys, P. (2006). *Towards a personalised educational landscape*. Retrieved 10 September 2006, from http://www.futurelab.org.uk/viewpoint/art80htm

Leadbeater, C. (2004). *Learning about personalisation: How can we put the learner at the heart of the education system?* Nottingham, UK: DfES/Demos. Retrieved 10 September, 2006 from http://www.demos.co.uk

Leadbeater, C. (2005). *The shape of things to come: Personalised learning through collaboration*. Nottingham, UK: DfES/National College for School Leadership. Retrieved 10 August 2006, from http://www.standards.dfes.gov.uk/innovation-unit

Leadbeater, C. (2006). The future of public services: Personalised learning. In Centre for Educational Research and Innovation, *Schooling for tomorrow: Personalising education* (pp. 101–114). Paris: OECD.

Lyotard, J-F. (1984). *The postmodern condition: A report on knowledge*. Manchester: Manchester University Press.

McKenzie, D. (1992). The technical curriculum: Second class knowledge? In G. McCullough (Ed.), *The school curriculum in New Zealand: History, theory, policy and practice* (pp. 29–39). Palmerston North: Dunmore Press.

McKinley, E., & Waiti, P. (1995). Te tauāki matauranga pūtaio: He tauira—the writing of a national science document in Māori. *SAME Papers* 1995, 75–95.

McLaughlin, M. (2003). *Tertiary education policy in New Zealand*. Wellington: Ian Axford Fellowhip in Public Policy.

Maharey, S. (2007). *Organising secondary schools for personalizing learning*. Speech notes for an address to the Auckland Secondary Schools Principals' Association. Retrieved 22 September 2007, from http://www.text.labour.org.nz/Our_mps_top/steve_maharey/speeeches_and_releases/070314/i

Meyer, L., McClure, J., Walkey, F., McKenzie, L., & Weir, K. (2006). *The impact of the NCEA on student motivation*. Wellington: Ministry of Education. Retrieved 16 July, 2007, from http://www.minedu.govt.nz/web/downloadable/d11337_v1/student-motivation-reportjune2006.doc

Miliband, D. (2004, January). *Personalised learning: Building a new relationship with schools*. Speech to North of England Education conference, Belfast, UK. Retrieved 16 July 2006, from http://www.publications.teachernet.gov.uk

Miliband, D. (2006). Choice and voice in personalised learning. In Centre for Educational Research and Innovation, *Schooling for tomorrow: Personalising education* (pp. 21–30). Paris: OECD.

Miller, R., & Bentley, T. (2003). *'Unique creation': Possible futures—four scenarios for 21st century schooling*. Nottingham, UK: National College for School Leadership/Demos.

Ministry of Education. (1992). *From 15 to 16: Raising the school leaving age*. Wellington: Learning Media.

Ministry of Education. (1993). *The New Zealand Curriculum Framework*. Wellington: Author.

Ministry of Education. (1996). *Te Whāriki: He whāriki mātauranga mō ngā mokopuna o Aotearoa—early childhood curriculum*. Wellington: Learning Media.

Ministry of Education. (1999a). A key point summary of the report of the Secondary Schools Sector Forum. *Achievement 2001*.

Ministry of Education. (1999b). Introducing the National Certificate in Educational Achievement: Developing Achievement Standards. *National Certificate in Educational Achievement*, 1(June).

Ministry of Education. (2000a). *National Certificate in Educational Achievement*. Report from Secondary Schools Sector Forum. Wellington: Author.

Ministry of Education. (2000b). *Report of the compulsory schools sector in New Zealand: Ngā kura o Aotearoa*. Wellington: Author.

Ministry of Education. (2004). *Ngā haeata mārautanga: Annual report on Māori education 2002–2003*. Wellington: Author.

Ministry of Education. (2005). *Key competencies in tertiary education: Developing a New Zealand framework—discussion document*. Wellington: Author.

Ministry of Education. (2006a). *Let's talk about personalizing learning*. Wellington: Author.

Ministry of Education. (2006b). *The New Zealand curriculum: Draft for consultation*. Wellington: Learning Media.

Ministry of Education. (2007). *Education statistics of New Zealand for 2006*. Data Management and Analysis Division (pp. 66–68). Wellington: Author.

Ministry of Education. (2007). *The New Zealand curriculum for English-medium teaching and learning in years 1–13*. Wellington: Learning Media.

Ministry of Education. (no date). *National Administration Guidelines*. Retrieved date from http://www.minedu.govt.nz/index.cfm?layout=document&documentid=8178&data=1

Nash, R. (2005). A change of direction for NCEA: On re-marking, scaling and norm-referencing. *New Zealand Journal of Teachers' Work*, 2(2), 100–106.

National Assembly for Wales. (2003). *Learning country: Learning pathways 14–19: Action plan*. Cardiff: National Assembly for Wales. Retrieved 8 June 2005, from http://www.learning.wales.gov.uk

New Zealand Government. (1999). *The national qualifications framework of the future: White paper*. Wellington: Ministry of Education.

NZQA. (2000). *University Entrance and the National Certificate of Educational Achievement: A consultation document prepared by the University Entrance Working Party*. Wellington: Author.

NZQA. (2001). Unit Standards and Achievement Standards. *QA News*, 38(June).

NZQA. (2004). *NZQA releases timeframe for planned UE standard review*. Retrieved 20 June 2005, from http://www.nzqa.govt.nz/news/releases/uereview.html

OECD. (2000). *Definition and selection of competencies (DeSeCo): Theoretical and conceptual foundations: Background paper*. Paris: Author.

OECD. (2002). *Definition and selection of competencies (DeSeCo): Theoretical and conceptual foundations: Strategy paper*. Paris: Author.

Pink, D. (2006). *A whole new mind: Why right-brainers will rule the future*. New York: Riverhead Books.

Popper, K. (1966). *The open society and its enemies: Volume one: The spell of Plato* (5th ed). London: Routledge & Kegan Paul.

Reid, W. (1987). The functions of school-based curriculum development: A cautionary note. In W. Reid (Ed.), *Partnership and autonomy in school-based curriculum development* (pp. 115–124). Sheffield: Education Division, University of Sheffield.

Renwick, W. (1986). *Moving targets: Six essays on educational policy*. Wellington: New Zealand Council for Educational Research.

Royal Commission on Social Policy. (1988). *The April report: Future directions and associated papers*. Wellington: Author.

Schwab, J. (1973). The practical: Translation into curriculum. *School Review, 81*, 501–522.

Scott, D. (2003). *Participation in Tertiary Education*. Wellington: Ministry of Education.

Senge, P., Cambron-McCabe, N., Lucas, T., Smith, B., Dutton, J., & Kleiner, A. (2000). *Schools that learn: A fifth discipline fieldbook for educators, parents, and everyone who cares about education*. New York: Currency/Doubleday.

Shacklock, G., Hattam, R., & Smyth, J. (2000). Enterprise education and teachers' work: Exploring the links. *Journal of Education and Work, 13*(1), 41–60.

Skilton-Silvester, P. (2003). Less like a robot: A comparison of change in an inner-city school and a Fortune 500 company. *American Educational Research Journal, 40*(1), 3–41.

Strachan, J. (2001). Assessment in change: Some reflections on the local and international background to the National Certificate of Educational Achievement (NCEA). *New Zealand Annual Review of Education, 11*, 245–273.

Tennant, M., & Yates, L. (2005). Issues of identity and knowledge in the schooling of VET: A case study of lifelong learning. *International Journal of Lifelong Education, 24*(3), 213–225.

Vaughan, K. (2003). Changing lanes: Young people making sense of pathways. In B. Webber (Ed.), *Educating for the 21st century: Re-thinking the educational outcomes we want for young people* (pp. 1–14). Wellington: New Zealand Council for Educational Research.

Vaughan, K., & Boyd, S. (2005). Pathways, junctions, and pitstops: Transition policy in New Zealand. In N. Bagnall (Ed.), *Youth transition in a globalised marketplace* (pp. 99–118). New York: Nova Science Publishers.

Vaughan, K., & Hipkins, R. (2007). *Learning to fly.* Unpublished paper.

Vaughan, K., & Kenneally, N. (2003). *A constellation of prospects: A review of STAR (the Secondary-Tertiary Alignment Resource).* Wellington: New Zealand Council for Educational Research.

Vaughan, K., Roberts, J., & Gardiner, B. (2006). *Young people producing careers and identities: The first report from the Pathways and Prospects project.* Wellington: New Zealand Council for Educational Research.

Warner, D. (2006). *Schooling for the knowledge era.* Camberwell, Vic: ACER Press.

Wylie, C., & Hipkins, R. (in press). *On the edge of adulthood: Young people's school and out-of-school experiences at 16.* Wellington: Ministry of Education.

Yates, L. (2006). Vocational subject-making and the work of schools: A case study. *Australian Journal of Education, 50*(3), 281–296.

Appendix A:
NCEA Achievement Standards
(as at November 2006)

Subject	Level 1	Level 2	Level 3
Accounting	x	x	x
Agriculture and horticulture	x	x	x
Art history		x	x
Biology	x	x	x
Chemistry	x	x	x
Classical studies		x	x
Dance	x	x	x
Drama	x	x	x
Economics	x	x	x
English	x	x	x
Geography	x	x	x
Graphics	x	x	x
Health	x	x	x
History	x	x	x
Home economics	x	x	x
Human biology	x		
Information management	x		
Languages generic	x	x	x
Latin	x	x	x
Mathematics	x	x	x
Media studies		x	x
Music	x	x	x
Physical education	x	x	x
Physics	x	x	x
Science	x	x	x
Social studies	x	x	x
Technology	x	x	x
Te reo Māori	x	x	x
Te reo rangatira	x	x	x
Visual arts	x	x	x

Appendix B:

Approved subjects list for entrance to university
(as at December 2005)

Approved subject	Field/Subfield/Domain/Standards
Accounting	Domain Accounting—Generic
Agriculture and horticulture	Domain Agricultural and horticultural science
Biology	Domain Biology
Chemistry	Domain Chemistry
Chinese	Domain Chinese
Classical studies	Domain Classical studies
Computing	Domain Generic computing
Cook Islands Māori	Domain Cook Islands Māori
Design (practical art)	AS90515, AS90516, AS90517, US9072, US9073
Drama	Subfield Drama
Economics	Domain Economics
English	Subfield English
French	Domain French
Geography	Domain Geography
German	Domain German
Graphics	Subfield Design
History	Domain History
History of art	Domain Art history
Indonesian	Domain Indonesian
Japanese	Domain Japanese
Korean	Domain Korean
Latin	Domain Latin
Mathematics with calculus	Domain Trigonometry, Domain Geometry, Domain Calculus, AS90638, AS90639, US5267, US11102, US12344
Statistics and modelling	Subfield Statistics and probability, AS90644, AS90647, US5256, US5264, US5262, US5272
Media studies	Domain Media studies
Music studies	Domain Music studies
Painting (practical art)	AS90659, AS90663, AS90667, US9066, US9067
Photography (practical art)	AS90660, AS90664, AS90668, US9064, US9065
Physical education	Domain Physical education
Physics	Domain Physics
Printmaking (practical art)	AS90661, AS90665, AS90669, US9069, US9068
Samoan	Domain Samoan
Science	Domain Core science, Domain Earth science
Sculpture (practical art)	AS90662, AS90666, AS90670, US9070, US9071
Spanish	Domain Spanish
Social studies	Domain Social studies
Te reo rangatira or te reo Māori	Subfield Reo Māori

www.ingramcontent.com/pod-product-compliance
Lightning Source LLC
Chambersburg PA
CBHW081332230426
43667CB00018B/2907